This book is dedicated to my dear Goomba, Tommy Magliozzi (Car Talk) and my dear wife, Ann Christy.

Contents

FOREWORD

Why would anyone want to read about me?

I ask myself this question, and then I laugh, because, as you'll discover I'm a tremendous narcissist, and of course, I already know the answer: Why *wouldn't* anyone want to read about me?!

Don't worry, I'm one of those good narcissists, one with a self-deprecating streak a mile long!

When I have a thought, I'm convinced it's the most original thought anyone's ever had. How could it not be? But then I start to wonder if my thoughts aren't so original after all, and maybe other people are thinking the same thoughts and asking the same questions about life and Divinity. Maybe I've just tapped into some wellspring of thought where all these questions and ideas foment, waiting for other questioning minds to latch onto them?

It's like Edison. When I think about the lightbulb, I remember that plenty of other inventors were working on the same concept at the same time. It's as if that chain of understanding was already in the broader consciousness, just waiting to emerge. Maybe it's the same with my insights about the Divine, about the afterlife, about the Trinity. Maybe my religious experiences aren't unique, but they are at least framed through my life, and told from the perspective of my experiences.

When he wrote about his experiences, Paramhansa Yogananda wrote about yogis from a yogi's perspective, and that made his groundbreaking work unique. It was the first book of its kind to reveal something about the journey towards something greater from one who had travelled every step of the way. Someone who'd seen it, done it, and bought the barabandi!

My own story—with a title that I've brazenly repurposed from Yogananda—is about transformation. About a kid from Boston's

North End who found enlightenment in lightning strikes and meditation benches, in street fights and sculpture, in love affairs and business ventures. It's about discovering that the path to wisdom isn't always straight, and sometimes the most profound truths come wrapped in the most unlikely packages.

Yogananda's name meant Divine union with God through Yoga. I can't claim that my name means anything so auspicious, but it reminds me of where I came from: the Catizone name originated in the Catanzaro province in the south of Italy. I am a proud Italian American, and, as you'll see, that fiery Italian blood runs through my family. And as for the yogi part? The key part of the yoga philosophy refers to someone who makes life choices that lead towards equanimity and inner peace, a balance I have striven to find—and to help other people find—throughout my life. So, I hope you'll indulge me for my little play on Paramhansa.

More prosaically, I've written this book because, as my 103-year-old grandfather from Naples used to say, "Pietro, you've got to talk about something." This is my something: a story about violence and peace, about performance and authenticity, about finding grace in the space between Christianity and Eastern spirituality. About learning that the Divine has a sense of humor, and that sometimes the most spiritual path is the one that makes you laugh. And so, I invite you to laugh too at stories of my ridiculous chutzpa and my even more ridiculous stupidity!

INTRODUCTION

<u>The Lightning Strike</u>

It was a long time since I had set foot in a church, but that summer afternoon, the compulsion was irresistible. St Stephen's Roman Catholic Church[1] in Boston's North End stood like a beacon against the piercing heat, proud and defiant against the changing mores of life in North End in the 1960s.

St Stephen's had been my parish church, the place where I'd rung the bells and received Holy Communion every Sunday. But I'd drifted away from church and dogma. It was the last place you'd expect to find a kid like me, mired in the violence of North End's streets. And yet, there I was, not knowing what I was doing there, or why I had come.

The heavy wooden door, worn smooth by generations of parishioners' hands, gave way to another world. The dim light and heavy, sweet air of lingering incense were in stark contrast to the fierce brightness outside. The silence enveloped me like a blanket, and I sank into a pew, utterly alone.

I must have sat there for an hour or more when I felt the atmosphere begin to change. Slowly at first, and then suddenly, as if someone had flipped a cosmic switch. The air grew charged with electricity. I could feel the prickling sensation running across my arms and down my neck, and I knew with absolute certainty what was going to happen next... The church was going to be struck by lightning. It wasn't an intuition; it was understanding beyond doubt.

---

[1] St. Stephen's Church, founded in 1875, was Boston's first Italian Catholic parish. Originally serving a predominantly Irish congregation, it became a cultural center for Italian immigrants after 1900. The church features the largest collection of religious-themed stained glass windows in New England.

Almost immediately, the stillness shattered. The church seemed to shake to its foundations as an explosion of light turned everything incandescent. Thunder roared overhead, so close it felt like it was inside my skull. There was no rain, just white-hot flashes of luminosity and crashes of sound that seemed to come from everywhere, all at once.

I sat transfixed, watching this Divine performance unfold around me. When I finally stepped outside, I emerged into a different world. The quiet street scene I had left was now a riot of blaring sirens and frantic activity. The church was surrounded by firemen and onlookers, all staring up at the steeple, wondering what they had witnessed. The sky above was still just as clear as it had been before I'd stepped inside.

I had gone into that church an angry young man, unsure of my place in the world. Hurt by the pain I had seen and experienced. But I woke up the next day a changed man. The violence that had coursed through my veins—inherited from generations of hot-blooded Italians, nurtured by the streets of the North End—was gone. I was transformed.

To understand that transformation—how lightning could burn away years of rage in a single moment—you need to understand where that rage came from. You need to know about the characters of North End: the comedians and Lotharios, the nutjobs and mafia men. But first, you need to know about my childhood—and especially my mother—and the particular brand of chaos she brought into my world...

PART I

BAPTISM BY FIRE

CHAPTER 1

<u>The Seeds of Violence</u>

"Where does all that violence go? Does it seep down into the next generation like poison in the groundwater? Where does it end?"

Minute by minute, I watched the slow arc of the sun as the light inched its way across my room. For eight hours, I sat there—alone and silent—of my own free will. I was just 12-years old, but even then, I felt the impulse coursing through me to reach beyond myself, to consider the big questions of life. The kinds of questions that weren't going to be answered by my teachers, or my family. Certainly not by my mother.

The attic room was my sanctuary, the one place I could escape the chaos below. From up there, I could hear the cacophony of North End drift up from the streets: the rapid-fire Italian, the arguments that sounded like murders being enacted, but were just conversations about dinner plans, the constant performance of life in the North End[2]. But in my room, watching that finger of light trace its path across the floor, I found a different kind of silence.

My mother would have been mystified by my stillness. She was never still. And it's fair to say she was not exactly blessed with a saintly nature. She was a Gemini, so she had two personalities: bad and worse. Violence wasn't just an occasional visitor to our home; it lived there, wore a dress, and put food on the table.

It's hard for anyone to believe just how angry and violent my mother could be. She was clever enough to fool people. Even to this day, I meet acquaintances who tell me I'm delusional, they tell me she was

---

[2] Boston's North End in the 1950s was home to approximately 60,000 people living in one square mile, making it one of the most densely populated Italian-American neighborhoods in the United States. By 1970, the Italian-American population would decrease to 40,000 as families moved to the suburbs.

a wonderful woman. But they never saw her wield a baseball bat at unsuspecting visitors she didn't like the look of. They never saw her take out her considerable anger on me. They never witnessed the way she could switch from charm to rage in an instant, like an actress changing costumes between scenes.

Maybe the violence was genetic. People would often comment on how different my brother and I were. He was about 15 years older than me, and we were opposites. He was like a mafia guy, he dressed the part, acted like one, and was very violent. My sister (10 years older than me) and my brother were always fighting. I remember one time she threw a knife at him, and it landed right between his eyes. It was, to put it mildly, a very violent household.

My maternal grandfather in Naples, who lived to the grand old age of 103, had been a very violent guy too. At fifteen, he killed a man in an argument over an olive tree. After that, he had to leave Italy in a hurry, and that's how he ended up in North End.

As a kid, I played with him, and joked around as kids do, without ever knowing my grandfather was a murderer. But even then, I could tell there was something about him. A line that I could never cross. I felt the same about my mother. She'd soaked up some of his violence like a sponge. As a young girl, she'd seen her father dragging her mother across the floor by the hair. And when my mother tried to intervene, he'd turned on her. My mother was only 13-years old when her mother died, and as the eldest of five siblings, she would be the one to get it when he needed to vent his rage on someone. She once told me how she would crawl under the bed to escape him.

Whenever they got together again in later life, they were like cats and dogs, always fighting. Ask my grandfather why my mother was the way she was, and he wouldn't have taken any responsibility for it. He always said it was because she'd tried to walk on a skylight as a child, and when the glass broke, she managed to grab on to the sides until she was pulled to safety. But she was left hanging there for several terrifying seconds, knowing that she would have plummeted several stories to her death. According to him, the horror of that experience explains why my mother acted like she did. He was secure in his belief that it was nothing whatsoever to do with the way he treated her.

The old Italians expected women to behave in a certain way, and if they showed any sign of disobedience, they were punished for it. And my mother, it seems, had been a particularly problematic child, and been punished accordingly.

My father's family was just as volatile. I experienced my paternal grandfather's temper at close range when I hit him on the head with a bowling pin. My mother had put me out on the fire escape at the front of the building, and my grandfather would stick his head out from his apartment, look down at me, and give me a wink. Now, I hadn't mastered the art of winking with one eye—he knew that and laughed at my efforts to wink back. The rage swelled up in me, and I grabbed a bowling pin that was lying around and threw it up at him. I couldn't have aimed it any better if I'd tried, and it hit him right on the top of his head.

In a white-hot rage, he came running down with my grandmother hard on his heels. He tried to grab me when my mother pulled me into one of the bedrooms and held the door closed from the inside. Standing fast in the doorway on the other side, my mother wouldn't let him get to me, it was the most courageous thing I ever saw her do. All his rage had to go somewhere—it wouldn't just dissipate—and he took it out on her instead. He punched her squarely in the face and gave her a black eye. His violence was legendary in our family.

Where does all that violence go? Does it seep down into the next generation like poison in the groundwater? Where does it end?

There was no violence in my father. He was a very gentle man, brilliantly clever. He invented all sorts of interesting machines, and he seemed a little more in touch with his feelings than my mother. I think my father loved me as far as his capacity to love allowed, be he wasn't a particularly demonstrative man. While he may not have been exuberantly affectionate, it was still more than my mother could manage.

My father had a brilliant mind, especially when it came to electronics. During the war, he created a device which he called 'The Magneto,' which was a wooden box with electronics inside it. By shooting electrical arcs through glass tubes, he was able to weld broken filaments back together, and he sold the repaired filaments to the military base on Commercial Street, at the end of Hannover Street. In the North End, during the second world war, they couldn't get the materials to make the vacuum filament tubes which were used for various wartime applications, including amplifying signals to detect low-flying planes, and creating radar images by generating radio-frequency power.

He understood electricity in a way that seemed almost mystical. Years later, when I asked him if he believed in God, he said, "No, I believe in vibration," which was essentially the string theory of Hinduism, though he wouldn't have known it that way. His insight came from working with electrical forces.

Like my father, I developed an odd relationship with electrical forces. Later in life, I could set off fax machines just by laughing. Once, standing in my kitchen with the windows closed, I called out to my UPS driver Tommy who was blocks away, and he turned his truck around, saying he'd heard me call his name. I've always had remote starters installed in my cars and one time, I managed to start my car by yelling at just the right frequency. My wife, Christy, watched it happen. It was as if that same electrical understanding my father had manifested differently in me.

My father even made his own pharmaceuticals, creating ointments that my aunt swore were more effective than anything doctors prescribed. But his brilliance never found its full expression. I once found tags in the basement that read 'Peter's Friendly Laundry' - just one of many businesses he tried. Initially, he put my mother out front to deal with the customers, but that just degenerated into scenes from *Fawlty Towers*, whenever my mother decided she didn't like a customer. In the end he told me, "I had to remove your mother in order to save the business!"

My father also fixed people's radios and TVs, but nothing quite stuck for him. My happiest memory of him is from my toddler years, and I was standing naked on the kitchen table. My father was sitting, eating eggs, and there was such a strange expression on his face. He was smiling at me. I had never seen that expression before; my mother never smiled. It was like seeing a rainbow in a storm—brief, beautiful, and rare.

I was always getting into trouble for mischief; I used to like cutting the electrical wires in our house, just for fun, but I don't remember my father hitting me out of anger or scolding me. There was just one time when my father had to pretend to hit me because he was supposed to, but he didn't hurt me.

I had been an unexpected child, arriving a full ten years after my sister. My brother still lived in the family home. Maybe you've heard that old joke that Christ must have been an Italian? There are three reasons why: For one, he believed his mother was a virgin. Two, his mother believed he was the son of God. And three, he didn't leave home until he was 33! My brother stayed in the family home until he was 40-years old, when he finally got married. But my mother had been too much for my father to cope with, and he left when I was just five years old.

He'd been holding down a job by day and studying to be a doctor by night, and the stress of it all was compounded by dealing with her. She made his life a living nightmare, and he just couldn't take it anymore. His dream of being a doctor had slipped away, and with it, something in him seemed to dim. I don't blame him for leaving. I would have left if I could have. But with my father gone, it meant that I was left alone with the lunatic that was my mother.

At this stage, you might be thinking that she couldn't possibly be as terrible as I've made out. But I don't think I've given you a real flavor of her particular brand of cruelty yet...

At 9-years old, I got polio. This was before the vaccine, and we didn't really know much about it. I came home with a splitting headache, and my back and neck were stiffening up. In response, my mother beat me. She beat me because I was sick, and that made her angry. It meant that she had to take care of me, and she didn't like being obliged to act like a mother. In the end, I cared for myself. When the pain was nearly unbearable, I discovered that if I covered my face with newspapers, it helped to ease it. Later, I learned that breathing in the carbon monoxide I'd exhaled helped to thin the blood and reduce the swelling.

At mealtimes, Mother liked nothing better than to start fights between me and my siblings. Then, when the fights were raging, she would just sit back, relax, and take a deep contented breath of enjoyment, revelling in the chaos that she had wrought. She was like a conductor of discord, orchestrating the mayhem with practiced skill.

Mother remained combative throughout her life. Years later, when we put her in a nursing home in North End, the psychiatrist asked me, "When did she get this way?" I told her, "She's always been this way!" She was shocked, "What... no medication, no psychiatric intervention – nothing?!"

And yet, my mother wasn't entirely without redeeming qualities. Her food was delicious. Anything cooked with real passion is only ever delectable... and she cooked with such unbridled hate! The house would be thick with the aromas of rich gravy on a Sunday, and I would sometimes try my luck and steal a meatball when she wasn't looking. Her meatballs were just so good that they overcame the fear of potential punishments. One of my friends tried Mother's meatballs and was still talking about it 20-years later.

My mistake was in trying to love my mother in spite of the horrors she visited upon me. I didn't know enough then to keep my peace. I was still laboring under the Christian edict that I had to show love, even when I was getting slapped in the face. And yet, in spite of her rage, and her brutality, she was just the kind of mother I needed. When Buddha realized Buddhism, it was because he left the safeness of the family compound into the world of misery. If Buddha had a happy soccer mom we would only have soccer.

With the omniscient power of hindsight, I can appreciate the vital role my mother played in sharpening my desire to move beyond my limited experience. Every moment of small realization in that attic room moved me further from the kinds of thoughts and desires that would normally have occupied a young child's mind. I grew accustomed to tuning out the mundane concerns of life in North End, to focus in on my breathing, and to ruminating on the questions that really mattered: How is the universe put together? What is truth? What is love?

I was looking for some kind of peace, trying to understand that I didn't want my happiness to be derived from who I thought I was, or who I thought I was supposed to be. I somehow understood there was power in controlling my breathing, and found my own technique. It felt intuitive, almost as if the knowledge had carried over from another life. It was blissful. I knew I was on the path to something revelatory.

But I was too wise too early; I couldn't escape my situation. At 7-years old, I couldn't leave my mother, or get out of the North End. But the impulse to keep searching for something *other,* something bigger, continued. It seemed to me as if there was another way of interpreting the world that would help me make sense of how I felt.

These kinds of outré thoughts didn't necessarily sit hand-in-glove with my upbringing. Being of Italian descent, Catholicism[3] was hardwired into me, and the presence of religion—if not the church as a body that we all attended—was a constant presence in all our lives. Saints and sinners alike, we all ended up at the same altar. Our community was a vibrant mix of devout and tempestuous people. I knew that same juxtaposition between the spiritual and the all-too-secular existed in me; I was a product of my family and my society, and that society was mired in violence.

One day, that violence would manifest in me too...

---

[3] Italian-American Catholicism in Boston was different from Irish Catholicism, incorporating traditions like the Feast of Saint Anthony and the Fisherman's Feast which combined religious devotion with secular festivities. Many families rented store fronts featuring saint's pictures, blessed palms, and religious artifacts. The practice of 'evil eye' protection (mal'occhio) persisted alongside orthodox Catholic practices, combining folk religion with more formal Catholic doctrine.

CHAPTER 2

<u>North End: A Fellini Film in Four Dimensions</u>

"In a world where you start out with nothing and have nothing to aspire to, pragmatism trumps virtue ethics."

The streets of North End moved to their own particular rhythm. A vivacissimo dance of passion. You could walk by blocks in the North End where every conversation sounded like a murder in progress. Hands waving in the air, voices rising and falling like grand opera, people screaming at each other over trivialities with the same intensity that non-North Enders might reserve for actual emergencies. In those days, they had a special law that if you were of Italian or Mediterranean descent, you would not be charged with verbal assault. It was understood that was just a part of the Italian psyche, particularly for the Southern Italians.

Violence in North End lived hand-in-glove with art, beauty, and of, course, Catholicism. People may have been devout and observant Catholics, but that didn't mean they couldn't also act in ways that were not mandated by the good book...

That sequence in The Godfather sums it up: in one scene, Michael is in church, baptizing his nephew, in the next, he's having the five major Mafia family heads murdered. Somehow, those two worlds co-existed without it feeling anomalous, we accepted that you could be a devout person who lived according to *most* of the Ten Commandments. You could be at church in the morning, singing of contrition and piety. And in the evening, you could be rubbing shoulders with hitmen.

It only added richness to our lives. It made the extremes more potent. It certainly put the absurdity of life into context. I can tell you that when you grow up in North End, you learn to find the humour in everything. And if you really want to get along, you learn how to make people laugh. Humour isn't just a way of life; it's a survival technique. It can save you from a beating, ingratiate you into the right people's company, or charm you into someone's bed.

Living alongside funny people and tough people is the best kind of preparation for life. Not wanting to fight any more than I had to, I quickly learnt how to make people laugh, and I've been making them laugh ever since.

Humor in the North End was often based around exposing people's flaws and quirks, giving everyone a nickname that stuck like dried spaghetti to a wall. There was Machine Gun Nick because he stuttered—ta-ta-ta-ta-ta-ta-ta-ta. One guy bought a beautiful pair of pants with a fine stripe down the leg. It was like the elevator operators used to wear, back when people would get into the elevator and say which the floor they wanted, and he'd operate the elevator for them. When he saw him, one of the guys shouted out "Two please" as if he was going to the second floor, and the name stuck.

We were more used to the nicknames than the real names. When somebody told me Johnny Scarbutio was in town, I didn't know who he was talking about. "Oh you mean Johnny Two-Shoes!" One kid had a deformity—one foot stuck out to the left and the other to the right—so we called him 10-15. In the North End, if you sneezed, instead of people saying "God bless you," they'd say, "Fuck you."

Even my mother had her own brand of humor; when she was in a nursing home in North End, she had a roommate with an unusually shaped head—it looked like an upside-down triangle. One day, I asked her what happened to her friend. She said, "Who? Hammerhead?" She had a way of seeing things so bluntly, like many Italians. I remember when we had Italian guests staying with us who talked about how, in Southern Italy, they'd put nicknames on tombstones. "Joey the Nose," or "Tommy Something-or-Other." It was hysterical to me.

You can tell a lot about a neighborhood by how it catalogued its characters. Some of the people I knew are long gone, some of their real names have been forgotten, but those nicknames are like a living archive. Every one of them tells a story and marked that person's place in the community.

Growing up in the North End was like living with an extended family—paisanos, goombas, cousins, second cousins, uncles. Everyone knew everyone else's business. The streets were our stage, walking down Hanover Street could take hours because you'd run into everyone, and everyone would want to talk to you. The street was alive with conversations, people yelling and gesturing, full of Southern Italian energy.

Let me tell you about some of the people with whom I shared the limelight of life in North End in the nineteen fifties and sixties. The roll call was vast. There was Norma Conte, one of the most unforgettable stars on the bill. She was a force of nature, a woman gangster with her own crew—stunningly beautiful in her youth, with curly blonde hair, piercing blue eyes, and dark, swarthy skin. Even the men were afraid of her, but although she had a tough-as-nails reputation, she liked me, and we got along well.

Once, I saw her at Whole Foods, where she casually told me, "My neighbors called the cops on me, and said my German Shepherd bit one of their family members... So I blew up their car." That was Norma. You didn't cross her. A restaurateur friend of mine, who wrote a book and openly mentioned guys like Vinny the Animal, wouldn't dare write about Norma. She was off-limits.

Inevitably, she spent time in prison. My friend Nick, an orthodontist, once had her in his dentist chair. As he reclined the chair, he noticed the crinkling of paper in her leotards. "Norma, what the hell is that?" he asked. She replied, "Oh, I just won $40,000 in the stock market." She was so off-hand about it.

Another time, I was at the Caffè Dello Sport (in their original location on Hannover Street) with some friends when Norma pulled up in her Mercedes. My friends were big celebrities in the area: Tom and Ray Magliozzi the MIT graduate grease monkeys! (Tom told me, he was accepted to both Harvard and MIT at the same time, the only reason he chose MIT, because it was $50 cheaper per year!) Their radio show,

Car Talk with Click and Clack[4], aired on National Public Radio from the seventies right the way through to 2012. What started out as a simple car show soon turned into a vehicle for their whip smart wit and drew fans from across the country. They were invited onto TV shows like Johnny Carson, Jay Leno, Letterman, the did Nova episodes, and were even invited by President Clinton to roast guests at his inauguration.

Of course, I went over to greet Norma and invited her to meet my friends. She scoffed and said, "Fuck them, come with me." And so of course, I apologized to Tom and Ray and went with her. They would have known that you didn't dare argue with Norma. We walked down Hannover Street to see her accountant, Tommy Nazaro, who handled finances for an eclectic mix of mob guys and restaurateurs. Tommy was a character himself—always dressed like Al Capone and every other word was 'fuck'. He had an office in a building he completely owned, with no other tenants. As we sat down, I noticed a gun on the desk next to me. I picked it up to examine it, and Tommy casually said, "Peter, when you're done, wipe your prints off that thing." That's the kind of world it was. You might not see a gun every day, in the same way that you might not see a prayer book every day, but they were both part of the fabric of North End, like the smell of sauce cooking, or the sound of church bells.

The streets had their own hierarchy of power. For decades, the Angiulo family had ruled North End's underworld. When the government finally took them down, some of the guys I'd grown up with were the next in line to take over, but they needed collateral. The main man was Vinnie Di Gangi, and he went to Sicily, to do a deal with his family's allies in Sicily. The deal was done, but there were complications. You can get the whole story from the man himself in Appendix 1.

Without the deal, and without the extra financial muscle it would

---

[4] *Car Talk* had approximately 3.3 million listeners per week at the time it ended its original run on radio, making it one of the most listened-to weekend radio programs in the United States. Ray's son, Drew, told me that Car Talk had about 10 million subscribers and of course millions more that listened to the show.

have brought, the guys' influence just petered out. Life could have been different had it been run by people who cared about the people of North End, but without the change in infrastructure, life slowly settled back into a piecemeal territory of every man and gang for themselves.

You have to understand that a lot of Italians are anarchists; they don't know how to work together. That's why Italy was so divided with all its different states. A friend of mine, Angelo, went to visit his hometown in Sicily, he said the people were running for Mayor—not just one or two of them, but practically everyone was running for Mayor!

The restaurants were at the heart of our neighborhood, and many of the restaurateurs were just as mad, band, and dangerous to know as any of the mob men. There was this one couple—he was from Naples, and she was from Abruzzi. They disliked each other but stayed married long enough to have kids. Then, they each ran competing restaurants right next to each other, using the same kitchen but refusing to speak. It was hysterical. But that's the kind of colorful dynamic that gave life in North End its piquancy.

The restaurants weren't just places to eat, they were stages where life's dramas played out. I was in a restaurant once where two chefs got into a fight, one chasing the other through the dining room with a knife. It may have looked wild to an out-of-towner, but we all just raised an eyebrow and got on with our meals. It was a normal part of our daily experience. Then there was the visiting Irishman making a scene about being cheated out of six dollars. The solution was simple enough, I walked over, handed him six bucks, and said, "Here, now let's all stop and enjoy our food." Drama defused, show over, time for dinner.

Music was everywhere. A guy called Charles Termini had a beautiful tenor voice but never trained it. One day, he stood in front of a butcher shop on Salem Street and belted out a stunning aria in the middle of the street before walking in to buy his sausages. I had two friends who were actually close to Andrea Bocelli and brought him to North End one summer evening. They were dining at a restaurant with the windows open when someone in the restaurant started playing Bocelli's music. Spontaneously, he stood up in the middle of the dining room and began to sing. The word spread quickly, and crowds gathered outside, drawn in by that luminous voice floating on the breeze.

Such sights and sounds, and unexpected interactions were all vibrant parts of the fabric of our daily lives. From living in other places over the years, I can't think of anywhere else quite like North End. Once, I helped an elderly Italian woman with something in her building. As we climbed the dark stairway, the space suddenly opened up, illuminating beautiful murals on the walls. Beauty hiding in plain sight, waiting to be discovered. They were a mix of Titian and Caravaggio, painted by one of her tenants. The sheer unexpectedness of that moment transcended the down-at-heel mise en scene. But that was the North End—and they were the contrasts that defined our neighborhood—violence and art, brutality and beauty, all coexisting in the same streets.

The old Italians were like living history books. Julio, for instance, was wonderful. When I was maybe 15, he would have been about 80. He would break down the differences between Italians with the precision of a cultural anthropologist. "Sicilians," he said, "are always working the deals, trying to figure out how to avoid hard work. The Abruzzese? They're hard workers and great cooks. The Napoletani," he'd say, "have the most beautiful dialect, which is why Naples has been the center of music for centuries." Unless you lived with those people, unless you *knew*, you might have dismissed his words as stereotypes, but those were the kinds of understandings that genuinely shaped how people interacted, who they trusted in business, or who they'd let their children marry.

I knew these men had wisdom, and I listened to them. I became close to a man named Nick Lauretano, the head engineer for the Army Corps of Engineers, and spent hours just listening to him talk about life and soaking up his knowledge. We talked about philosophy— Plato, Socrates—he was a great thinker. I was completely engrossed in his ideas, and it felt like a privilege to learn from all the other guys who had truly lived their lives, rather than just existing through their lives as so many people did. I soaked up all the influences that came my way: philosophy, music, humor, and all the lessons of the streets. Lessons in honor, enmity, and vengeance...

In North End, even grudges could be elevated to an art form. Take Vinnie's records... Vinnie Di Gangi's mentor, Ermenio Forziati, a fellow Italian and music enthusiast, had promised Vinnie his prized record collection upon death. When the time came, Vinnie delivered a heartfelt eulogy for his late friend, but when it came to it, his family held onto the records for themselves.

Four decades later, Vinnie returned to the North End from Florida. One of his first stops was to see me. "I need your help with something," he said. "I'm paying a visit to Fazio about those records. I want what's mine." In the North End, a promise is a promise, even if it takes half a lifetime to see it honored.

Vinnie had tracked down the collection, now stashed in Fazio's basement. We went to see Fazio at his restaurant, and made him an "offer he couldn't refuse." Eventually, Fazio agreed to take us to his house, where the records were stored. Armed with cardboard boxes we taped together on Salem Street, we had Fazio haul up the heavy collection—nearly 100 pounds of records—and fill the boxes for Vinnie.

We went over to our friend Tony Checca's house and sorted through the records. But the vultures had already picked over the bones of the collection and there were only a couple of interesting items left. You might have thought Vinnie would have been furious at being denied his bequeathed prize, but for him, it wasn't about the records. It had never really been about the records, it was about righting a wrong. About seeing an agreement honored. It was that classic North End mentality: you don't forget, and you don't let things go.

Vinnie's tells a great story about some Irish tourists which illustrates the way we did things in North End. He tells how he stumbled across these tourists, who were looking for recommendations for ways to spend their time in the area. Being the perfect gentleman, he recommended his favorite restaurant. Sure enough, when he went there that night, he saw them and went over to say hello. It was all very convivial. But then, word got back to him that one of them made a crack about Italian women having mustaches. Vinnie was incensed, and plotted with the restaurant owner to teach them a lesson in respect. They went over to the table, armed with empty bottles, primed to smash them over the guests' heads. At the last moment, the Irish man understood his faux pas, made a very panicked apology, and they were able to stay and enjoy their desert, rather than having to take it to go in an ambulance.

Our neighborhood had its own internal laws. The official word of law nominally governed our behaviour, but it was really much too inflexible for us. Being born in North End gives you an innate sense of how the law works for you and yours. We all knew that you could drive the wrong way down a one-way street if you were sufficiently well connected. Or you could double park if you knew the right people. But break an unwritten rule, like disrespecting someone's mother or parking in their spot, and no connection in the world could save you.

None of this is meant to suggest to you that the North End was just about violence and vendettas. To me, it was more about performance. Life played out on the streets and in the restaurants in little vignettes of everyday melodrama. In the midst of all the febrile excitement and life-or-death scenes, music would suddenly emerge, transforming the ordinary into something magical.

Walking down Hanover Street you'd pass in and out of a hundred little dramas and comedies: past Norma in her Mercedes, past Tommy Nazzaro's office with its casual display of weapons, past Charles Termini singing his arias. Past restaurants where chefs might be fighting in the kitchen, or Andrea Bocelli might be giving an impromptu concert in the dining room. Past old timers like Julio, teaching the next generation about the subtle distinctions between Italian regions and temperaments.

In this theater of life, we all had our roles to play. Some, like Vinnie waiting forty years to reclaim his records, played the long game. Others, like the warring restaurant couple, performed their daily drama of spite and shared space. It was a world of characters all believing themselves to be the stars in their own operas.

But I think that to truly understand how this world shaped those of us who grew up in it, you have to start with a child's-eye view of the streets. You have to understand what it was like to watch and learn, to absorb these lessons of love and violence, of honor and revenge, of family and fear. You have to understand what it meant to be a kid in a world where everything—even slashing tires—was taught as if it were an art form to be mastered.

CHAPTER 3

Before the Lightning

"I ran with the gang, but there was something in me that held back from complete surrender to violence."

I went to high school in a pretty rough area with lots of projects, gangs, and violence. As far as racial harmony went, it was a pretty discordant area, put it that way. If you looked at someone the wrong way, you could end up in a fight. If you had the wrong face (or the wrong color face) you could end up in a fight. If you went out of your way to try and avoid trouble, you could end up in a fight. (You get the idea.)

The rumors had it that I was one of the toughest guys in the North End. I was a street fighter, true, but I wasn't a Rocky Marciano type, and I didn't get involved in too many fights directly. I was funny enough and tough enough to encourage most of the other kids to just let me be. When I did get involved, it was usually for someone else's benefit. Like when a fight broke out outside the school between a couple of mismatched guys; one of them was huge and the other one was a bully's wet dream. I didn't know either of them, but I stepped in and stopped it. Of course that didn't sit well with the bigger guy, and he decided to come after me later.

By the time he caught up with me a few days later, we were in one of the more civilized areas of Boston, far away from North End. He advanced on me, monkey wrench in hand, ready to unscrew my head from my shoulders. And that's when someone in the crowd stepped in—a guy from my neighborhood called Puopolo. He was known to be a little unhinged and pretty violent himself, but as a fellow North End guy, he was sold on my reputation. Most of all, Puopolo liked the fact that I stood up to people who needed to be stood up to.

He got between us and simply said, "I wouldn't do that if I were you!"

The guy froze. You could see the hesitation in his eyes as if he was suddenly questioning everything. Was there something he didn't know? Did I have backup or a weapon? Puopolo didn't explain; he just let the doubt hang in the air. One monkey wrench was never going to be enough for two of us, and the bully backed off.

Inevitably, I found my way into the gangs. One of them was called the Invaders. It still feels wrong to speak of everything we used to do back then, but it's fair to say that our activities ran the gamut of antisocial behaviours. They used to joke that kids in North End earned their doctorates in slashing car tires. And we certainly slashed a few in our time. The North End was notorious for people owning their parking spaces, and if someone parked where they shouldn't park, they'd reap the consequences. That was just a given. And too bad if it happened to someone who just didn't know the rules.

I had my own particular technique for slashing a tire more efficiently. Most people would swing a stiletto blade, ice pick, or something sharp at the tire, but that often caused the tool to bounce back. My method was different. Instead of striking, I would rest the blade gently on the tire, then use my other hand to push it in firmly. No bouncing, no drama, just precision. It was an efficient and subtle technique, you might almost say it spoke of some untapped artistry.

Slashing tires enabled us to mete out justice on the streets, playing judge, jury and executioner, exacting vengeance on anyone who deserved it. There was an almost covert, calculated nature to it, not unlike terrorism. No one knew where we'd strike. We were so good that we could do it in their line of sight. And the chutzpa of doing it in plain view made it even more thrilling. The performative element of it excited me most of all. Even years later—and even after all the changes in my life—that imperative to hand out my own kind of justice stayed with me. There was a time, long after I should have given up slashing tires when the impulse was just too strong...

I wasn't in a good mood. I'd got involved in a business deal that hadn't gone so well, I'd lost a fair bit of money, and I was hurting in a way that the pain could only really be satisfied with violence. I was on my way out of the North End, and some guy cut me off, and gave me the finger for good measure. As if that wasn't bad enough, he had some stupid bumper sticker that really pissed me off: *You can take my wife, but you can't take my dog!* That was enough to raise my hackles, but I took a few deep breaths, tried to let it go, and carried on my way out of town.

By the time I got to Cambridge, I was still in a pretty emotional state, still smarting from losing my money, and still seething about being cut off and flipped off. I could stand just about anything except injustice, especially injustice enacted against me! So, I was entering a turnaround, and another guy started to pass me by. I was a good distance away from him, and respectfully holding back until he'd passed, not wanting to let the other incident incite me. And then, as he levelled with me, he stared straight at me and gave me the finger.

As you'll discover, I was a very different man from the angry kid on the streets by that point, but that was one injustice was too much. You can only push Peter Catizone so far, and you can only rely on his beneficent nature for so long…

So, I followed the guy, not caring whether he noticed me or not. I watched him park, and slid in right behind him. I watched him get out of his car, and I could tell by watching the way he moved that he was a martial arts guy. He was lithe on his feet, flexing his muscles as he walked. So, of course, I exacted justice in the time-honored tradition; I slashed his tires, and then I went for an espresso at Café Paradiso in Harvard Square. Calmer, but not yet sated, I decided that that I was going to return to the scene of the crime to watch him. I sat in my car and enjoyed every single second of him realizing what had happened, and then struggling to sort it all out. He could clearly see me, just watching, not once offering to help, and so, justice was served.

Of course now, I feel sorry for it. Sorry for those things I did. Or at least most of them. Some of them were done in the heat of the moment. Some of them seemed to be written into my operating code in such a way that I couldn't have not done them. And some of them were necessary steps along the path to a different way of understanding and interacting with my world.

But back in my childhood, when I was living life in a living, breathing Fellini movie, the rules were different. The violence went beyond the sordid sort of everyday concerns into something almost operatic in its intensity. I wasn't the only kid starring in those scenes, I rubbed shoulder-to-shoulder with a cast of characters who all had their starring roles, their entrances and exits. And some of their stories were even more violent than mine.

People would get into fights over nothing. I knew a guy who killed his best friend's brother over a parking space. And if that isn't sufficiently insane for you, consider this: he shot him in the stomach so it wouldn't hurt so much. He may have wanted him dead, but that didn't mean he had to be an animal about it. You put an overture on that, throw the North End kids into their roles, and it just plays out like grand opera.

Our gang had a reputation for violence that was well deserved. We had pitched battles in the street with other gangs and ran riot across town. We could have been ripped from the pages of William Foote Whyte's *Street Corner Society*[5]; the corner boys and college boys at the opposite ends of our world.

The gang had members with different levels of commitment to the cause. Some guys were in it purely for protection, it was easy to feel inured to the violence of North End when you ran with the tough guys. Some guys were there for the thrill of it. Then there were those who were just looking for somewhere to belong. And at the top of the tree were the Bonafide tough guys. Two of them, Carlino and Volpe, ended up being surrounded by guys from a Boston gang on one misjudged foray into enemy territory. They were hopelessly outnumbered, and the kicks and punches were raining down on them. Our guys just put themselves back-to-back, and took 'em all on. The pile of unconscious bodies just grew at their feet until they'd wiped them all out.

One time, we set forth with the zest of our young years to go and 'act the maggot' in the Irish neighborhood. Armed with cherry bombs, we

---

[5] William Foote Whyte's "Street Corner Society" (1943) was a groundbreaking sociological study of Boston's North End. Whyte lived in the neighborhood for three years, documenting the social structures of Italian-American street gangs and social clubs. His work remains a seminal text in urban ethnography.

rained down our mischief, and were soon being chased out of town by the Charlestown Police. They caught up to us on the bridge. Their paddy wagon rumbled one way, and we ran the other. Back and forth we went, keeping out of their way, just prolonging the agony.

I'd barely stopped running, but when I saw the police catch the first of my friends, I gave up and walked back towards them. I wasn't about to let my friends go down without me. And that's when he pounced: a monstrous giant of a policeman grabbed me. He evidently thought that because I'd been so eager to keep running, I must be the weak link. He was big enough to lift me wholesale, and he carried me over to the parapet and then hauled me over the edge of Charlestown Bridge.

I swayed in his grip, knowing that with a twitch of his fingers, or a lapse in concentration, I'd be plummeting towards the water, but I wasn't remotely scared. The wind was whistling in my ears, and he was roaring—even louder— "If you don't tell me which one of you had the explosives, I'm dropping you."

I wasn't swayed. I knew he wasn't going to let go, and I calmly said, "I'm not telling you." With some regret, he put me back down on the ground, and we were all put into the back of the paddy wagon and taken to the police station. There, they bundled us out, and everyone was led off, except me. Thinking he'd have another crack at me, the same cop took me round to the back of the station. He cornered me between a couple of lockers and pushed me up against the masonry wall. Very deliberately, he took off his jacket, slowly rolled up his sleeves, and said, "I'm going to beat the fucking shit out of you if you don't tell me which one had the bombs." Calm as you like, I said, "I'm not going to tell you." Eventually, he rolled his sleeves back down, put on his jacket and took me back to the others. He said, "You've got a good friend here." My friends knew I would never have betrayed them. We were brothers. Standing up to authority and protecting your own were cardinal virtues in the North End.

As my reputation grew, so did the whispers going around that I was one of the toughest guys in the North End. Every fight, every confrontation with the cops, every moment I had to prove myself on the streets—it all felt like it was leading somewhere, but I didn't know where. People were starting to see me as something I wasn't sure I wanted to be. The reputation I'd built without knowing it, was becoming a cage. People expected certain things from me: the tough guy from the North End, the kid who wouldn't break under pressure. Even the cops were treating me differently after the Charlestown bridge incident. That kind of defiance— refusing to give up my friends even after being held over the edge of the bridge—earned respect, even from the people who were supposed to be controlling us. But respect in the North End came with expectations. The better your reputation, the more you had to live up to it.

Every encounter with the police only enhanced my reputation still further. So, inevitably, I was accompanied home by cops on a few occasions, and with my father gone, my brother often took on the role of disciplinarian. He would slap me around just enough to prove to the watching police that I'd been taught an appropriate lesson.

It would have taken a lot more effort to slap the violence out of our community. Still today, people tell me how North End's reputation for violence was legendary. One of our Vietnamese mechanics once told me how back in the day, Vietnamese criminals had tried to infiltrate the States, but the Italian mafia cut them to pieces and sent their body parts back to their families in Vietnam. That's how brutal it was.

As the years passed, the scope and scale of the violence didn't change much, even if our clothes did. By my mid-teens, we cut a more stylish look in our sports coats – more Droog than Sharks. We looked like gentlemen, even if we didn't act like the sort of gentlemen a young lady might want to take home to meet her mother. The violence was still there, but now it wore better clothes.

But even in the midst of gang life, something set me apart. Some guys in the Invaders seemed to live for the next battle, the next chance to prove themselves. I could hold my own, but there was always something in me pulling me in a different direction. Maybe it was those hours I spent as a kid, sitting alone in my room, watching the sun track across the floor, thinking about bigger questions than who controlled which street corner.

While I could fight as well as any of them, I wasn't consumed by violence the way some of them were. I ran with the gang, gladly, but there was something in me that held me back from complete surrender to brutality. It was as if I didn't want to be violent, but that never felt like a choice I could ever make for myself. The violence was deep inside me, imprinted on my DNA. And I could no sooner have rid myself of that part of myself than I could have changed my eye color...

There were times when I teetered on the edge of spiraling further into violence, but something always held me back. I got into an argument with someone once, and he was pushing all the wrong buttons. I could feel the rage simmering, until it bubbled over, and I lashed out. I grabbed him, got my hands around his neck and nearly squeezed the life out of him. He fell to the floor choking and blacked out. I actually thought I'd killed him and left him there on the street, the rage blinding me to the consequences. Bear in mind, this wasn't an enemy or a rival gang member, this was a friend! We became friends again later, but he was always more wary around me and definitely watched my hands after that.

There were just a couple of times when I'd got someone on the ground and my knees were on their shoulders and I just beat the shit out of them... but then, at the last moment, I'd stop. You could call it compassion or conscience; I just couldn't take advantage of someone who was that vulnerable. And afterwards, I was always terrified, not just because of what I'd done, but because of the realization that the violence in me lived so close to the surface.

You could say that at fifteen, everything feels like life and death, but in the North End, it really was like that. I knew I was capable of dangerous levels of violence. I could feel it in me, like a storm building. The same blood that had driven my grandfather to kill a man over an olive tree, and made my mother take a baseball bat to unsuspecting visitors-that was my inheritance, as much a part of me as my name. Was my propensity for violence more evidence of my mother's influence, and of my hot-blooded Italian ancestry coursing through me. I ran into a Sicilian friend of mine and my propensity for violence made perfect sense to him. He shrugged, and said, "That's just how the Sicilian roll."

It could equally have been the spicy combination of too much testosterone in a permanently combustible environment. Whatever it was, when riled, I was a match for anyone. It helped that people underestimated me. I was so softly spoken, it didn't compute that I had such violence in me. I'm not saying I went around talking about fava beans and a nice chianti, but I unnerved people just the same. When you get in someone's face, and ever so quietly tell them you're going to dismember them, they tend to accept it as fact and back off.

But there was something else too. The streets of North End had raised me tough, but my own questing mind was already thinking, questioning, and looking for something more. Running with the Invaders, I was caught between wanting to prove myself on one hand, and, on the other, wanting to explore the deeper part of me, the part that kept pulling back. I wasn't the only one who noticed the duality. Even some of the older guys would look at me sometimes like they were seeing something they didn't quite understand. Here was this kid who could fight with the best of them but who somehow seemed to be walking a different path.

Something had to give. You can only live with that kind of tension for so long before something breaks. I was tough enough and funny enough to maintain my place in the hierarchy, but inside, the conflict was becoming unbearable. It felt as if something had to give.

Years later, in meditation, I had a dream that helped me understand this duality. In the dream, three men were trying to kill me with guns. I killed all three, and only after the last one fell could I enter a deep meditative state. I realized I was killing aspects of myself and the violence that stood between me and enlightenment. I was reminded of the World War II veterans who said the biggest assholes often turned out to be the ones who'd save your life. Maybe those contradictions served some purpose. Perhaps there was value in knowing the capacity for violence and the capacity for protection came from the same source.

I didn't know it then, but I was about to experience something that would change everything. The violence that had been bred into my bones, passed down through generations of hot-blooded Italians, was about to meet a force more powerful than any I'd encountered on the streets.

CHAPTER 4

The Transformation

"Everything stopped. The silence was absolute. And then, the world exploded in a beam of pure radiant light."

The sky was perfectly clear. The sort of clarity that reveals the world in all its infinitesimal beauty. When you feel as if the veil has been lifted, and you can see behind the artifice of the truth that hides underneath everyday life.

I can't tell you what drew me to St Stephens Roman Catholic church[6] that day. My days of learning catechism and scripture were behind me, and it was a very long time since I had set foot in there. My world had expanded and contracted: my mind at once full of the violence of the streets, and the sanctity of my own spiritual path. Catholicism and its dusty doctrine had nothing to say to either side of me.

I don't know how I found myself to be there. I had no other business in that part of town. And if you had asked me how or why I had got there, or what I meant to do there, I could not have told you. But as I stood, quite motionless, as life on the streets continued around me, I could almost feel real life melting away, until all that remained, all that I could fix my eyes upon, was that church.

I moved across the road, hardly aware of traffic, stretched out my

---

[6] St Stephen's stood at the heart of our neighborhood, its bells marking time as they had for generations. I'd walk past it sometimes, remembering when I used to ring those bells, when I'd take Holy Communion and try to remember the Act of Contrition in the confessional booth. Back then, my biggest worry had been forgetting the words, making up sins on the spot when my mind went blank. Now my sins were real enough.

hand toward the heavy wooden door, worn smooth by generations of parishioners' hands, and pushed... Like an abrupt transition in a film, everything changed. The cool, dark, incense-perfumed interior of the church swallowed me up. It didn't just feel like a different world, but a different kind of world. Something other. Free of the kind of violence and testosterone-fueled fury of my world, it was like the calm of meditation.

And, as if in a meditative state, time passed me by. My world became one of absolute silence and stillness. But then, almost imperceptibly at first, I felt the change in the air. An electrical charge. I felt for a second as if the current ran up and down my body, almost as if it was searching for something inside me.

Just as suddenly, the prickling across my skin stopped. Everything stopped. The silence was absolute. And then, the world exploded in a beam of pure radiant light.

I intuitively knew the church had been struck by lightning. A moment later a thundercrack roared overhead. The light levels remained undimmed. No clouds passed overhead. No rain fell. But for a moment the sky above the church felt as if it was being torn asunder by sound and radiance.

Nothing about it made any sense, but I was completely untroubled by it. In the aftermath, I sat in reverence. Not of God, but of the transformative power of change. Of transfiguration, the Catholics might call it.

After a few more moments, I got up and stepped back into that other world, a different person. The mortal world I had left to go into the church was just as bright and clear. No clouds stormed the sky. There had been no rain. But the scene was otherwise completely changed. I emerged, as if from the scene of some natural disaster. All around me sirens blared, and firefighters ran about me. Crowds of onlookers had gathered, all looking up at the steeple, not knowing what they had witnessed.

I slipped through the crowds, and walked home. Just as I could not have recounted to you any details of my journey to the church, so I could not have told you anything of my journey home. I know only that I was changed. The violence that had coursed through my veins—inherited from generations of hot-blooded Italians, nurtured by the streets of the North End—was gone.

Later, when I mentioned this to my friend Mary Fisher, an Egyptologist and a scholar of the Old and New Testaments, she said, "Peter, the lightning was a baptism. Moses was baptized by fire with the burning bush, and you were baptized by lightning."[7]

I never thought of it that way, but it made sense. When God transforms someone in scripture, it's often through elements—fire, water, light. Moses had his burning bush, Saul was struck blind by Divine light on the road to Damascus, Christ was baptized in the Jordan. My transformation came through lightning, nature's own Divine fire. And the fire of brutality in me felt like it had been transformed into something else, something that could warm rather than burn.

At fifteen, I was just beginning to understand how profound the change had been. The North End was still the North End, with all its dramas and violence, its feuds and vendettas. But I was different. Something fundamental had shifted inside me, opening up possibilities I hadn't known existed.

I didn't know then where this transformation would lead me, what

---

[7] The concept of baptism by fire appears throughout Biblical and theological traditions. The burning bush episode (Exodus 3:1-4:17) represents Moses' Divine calling and initial encounter with God. Baptism by fire is more commonly associated with the Holy Spirit, particularly in the New Testament. The phrase "baptism of fire" originates from Matthew 3:11 and Luke 3:16, where John the Baptist declares: "I baptize you with water for repentance, but he who is coming after me... will baptize you with the Holy Spirit and fire." Baptism by fire involving a Divine presence manifesting through fire, serves as a moments of spiritual transformation, and mark the beginning of a Divine commission. It is said that the burning bush represents how the Divine can transform without destroying.

doors it would open, what paths it would set me on. I only knew that everything had changed, and there was no going back to who I had been before the lightning struck[8].

---

[8] The Catholic Church maintains records of significant events affecting church property. Archival documents record that St. Stephen's Church was struck by lightning in the mid-1960s, and no structural damage was recorded.

CHAPTER 5

The Wiseguy Whisperer

"When the violence left me, the touch of kindness felt revelatory. It was a much more powerful feeling than anger."

After the lightning strike, people noticed the change in me immediately. They asked me, "What happened? I couldn't explain it. How do you describe a transformation that you don't fully understand yourself? I knew only that I had gone into the church as one person and emerged another. The violence that had coursed through my veins—inherited from generations of hot-blooded Italians, nurtured by the streets of the North End—was gone. The neighborhood was the same. The violence was still there, woven into the fabric of daily life. But I saw it differently now, and more importantly, I reacted to it differently. That same blood still coursed through my veins, but it no longer carried that burning need for violence.

That's not to say that navigating the change was easy. When a reputation has grown up around you as someone not to be messed with, people don't just let you walk away from that. They test you, probe for weakness. But somehow, the very calmness that had come over me became its own kind of strength. People didn't know what to make of it. Perhaps because it seemed so anachronistic, so *other*.

When the violence left me, the touch of kindness felt revelatory. It was a much more powerful feeling than anger or any inclination towards violence. I started to see the smallest examples of kindness everywhere I looked. I realized that they'd been going on all around me without me even noticing.

I saw a guy I vaguely knew, called Mr. White, just going about his business. He was a busy, big-company guy, and I just saw him stop and talk to a little old lady in the street. That one little moment shone like a precious diamond to me. It was just a casual act of kindness, but it was something I had never ever seen before, and it touched me deeply. Seeing moments like that happening all around me changed my perspective and helped shape the person I wanted to be.

And then, late one night, I saw a black guy being set on in the street by three guys. By the time I got close enough to help they had already run off into the darkness with his wallet, but I wanted to make sure they hadn't hurt him too badly. He was sitting on the curb and after I'd checked him over, I said, "Let me replace the money they took from you."

As I said it, he looked into my eyes, and I could see that he had used to be somebody special, or important, or deeply spiritual. There was a certain ethereal look about him, and I felt almost as if our souls touched. He told me not to worry, and I felt instantly comforted. It seemed as if he had something better than money, as if he had some spiritual comfort. Being open to seeing and experiencing these moments happening all around me made my world spin. It felt like all sorts of new possibilities were opening up to me.

Growing up, it had always seemed that you had to pick a specific model if you wanted to fit into 'the system'. As if life gives you all these tailored suits to choose from, each one representing a person you can choose to be, and a path you can take, according to the conventional mores of life's dance. It seemed to me as if some of my friends had been woven into their suits for life, and like it or not, their courses were set. It didn't matter who they wanted to be, or who they could have been, because they were born into a certain family, it looked as if their future was already established.

My future was more mutable than most of the guys I knocked around with, and I wanted to explore the limits of my horizons. That didn't just extend to my position in life, but to my thinking on deeper realities.

Being born into Catholicism is almost as hard to escape from as being born into the Mafia. Whatever went on at home, whatever fresh hell my mother visited upon me, she still held to Christian doctrine, even if she was just a Christian in name only. She didn't often go to church unless she wanted to show off an expensive new outfit. As a child, I went along to church with my young friends, and I would ring the bells, and take Holy Communion and confession. I could never quite remember what was supposed to happen in the confessional booth. You'd have to recite the Act of Contrition, while the priest spoke in Latin from the other side of the confessional booth. The whole thing made me so nervous that I'd forget everything I was supposed to say.

Sometimes, I'd make up sins on the spot: "Oh, I lied," or "I did this or that." None of it was true—I'd just go completely blank once I got in there.

One time, I tried imitating the priest's Latin mumbling, and he suddenly yelled out in his thick Irish accent, "What are you, a wise guy?"

"No, Father," I stammered, "I just forgot the Act of Contrition, that's all." Even then, I was learning how to perform to get some attention.

As any Catholic should, I learned all about original sin, and felt a certain attraction to the focus on suffering in Christianity. Perhaps it felt appropriate to my own situation in life.

When I read the New Testament of the Bible, a lot of the things that Christ said really resonated with me. And I could get right behind the emphasis on love, but still, it didn't *feel* right. It was just too rigid in its doctrines. Most of all, the concept of the Saints – who were presented as near-perfect individuals – didn't really fit into my world view.

It occurred to me that if my sin was already pre-established, and I was going to purgatory whatever happened, it didn't leave Catholicism much capacity to inspire me. And on that basis, I was more than happy to accept Spinoza's thinking that 'there is no post-mortem realm of reward and punishment'. Pure Catholicism didn't seem like a good fit. But that didn't mean that some augmented form of Catholicism couldn't work…

Rather than fearing other religious ideologies, I started to see instead how other routes to what was essentially the same end could complement Catholicism, and that is when things started to connect for me. I'd been fascinated by my experiments at controlling my breathing, realizing how my consciousness changed as my focus on my breathing intensified. I hadn't known anything about the focus on

36

the breath in Hinduism and Buddhism, until I started to look beyond the Bible, and my reading of the Bhagavad Gita.[9] The fuel in my spiritual booster rockets was building, preparing me to take off into other realms of understanding. I was changing.

The wiseguys[10] of North End certainly noticed. The guys I'd seen with that certain untouchable aura—the people that everyone steered clear of—started to seek me out. They knew I'd been a tough kid, and they knew that I was probably heading in the same direction as them. But that wasn't what drew them to me, they came because they'd heard there was something different about me. That I was somehow changed, and they wanted to see it for themselves.

The first time it happened, one of them tracked me down in a dark corner at the gym. I was scared out of my wits thinking I'd found my way onto somebody's hitlist and he was coming to make the hit. It was a guy I only knew by reputation, and that reputation was a big enough red flag. But there was something in his manner and his awkward small talk that made me realise this was something else entirely. He fumbled through an awkward conversation starter and then came out with it, "I wanted to talk to you about... what it means to live a good life..."

After that, more of them came to see me with their questions, their doubts, their spiritual yearnings. These were men who lived by violence, yet here they were, asking me—still just a kid—about other

---

[9] In the Bhagavad Gita, the control of breath (pranayama) is discussed as a fundamental practice of yoga, particularly in Chapter 4, verse 29 and Chapter 5, verses 27-28. Krishna describes how controlling the inward and outward breaths leads to equilibrium of consciousness and spiritual awakening. This ancient Hindu text teaches that conscious breathing serves as a bridge between body and mind, enabling practitioners to achieve higher states of awareness—a concept that parallels meditative practices found across various spiritual traditions.

[10] In case you're wondering, the term "wiseguy" originated in the 1940s as street slang for a made member of the Mafia. By the 1960s, it had become a common euphemism in Italian-American communities for anyone connected to organized crime.

ways of understanding the world. They knew at least that I had been one of them – a tough kid who had grown up on the same streets, so I already had their respect.

You couldn't help but feel affection for them. In spite of everything they'd seen and done, their empathy and their humanity still shone though. A guy called Sal would speak in whispers about Eastern teachings, trying to reconcile his Catholic upbringing with his hunger for something more. He knew it didn't fit the stereotype for him to express an interest in Eastern teaching. After all, he was a good hitman *and* a good Catholic! But he opened up his heart to the possibilities of a different life. It was a beautiful thing.

It struck me as remarkable how these hardened men would let their guards down when they talked about spiritual matters. They'd been raised Catholic, but many of them felt trapped by its rigid doctrines. When I talked about other paths to understanding God through meditation and breathing techniques, and Eastern spirituality, their eyes would light up with possibility.

I was like the 'Wiseguy Whisperer'. Because I was accessing other ways of thinking, I could impart some kind of peace to those guys. I could let them expound their own ideas and help them to embrace ideas from beyond the lessons they'd learned at school, or in St. Stephen's. I could show them a way to accept themselves while still seeking something better.

Guys who had routinely fought and killed were now asking me questions about peace and redemption. As my relationship with these men grew deeper, more of them came into my orbit. They all had their own demons to face, and they came in search of some deeper spiritual conversation about the things they'd done. There I was, a teenager, fraternizing with some of the most violent men in our society, but it didn't seem strange to me. They had always been there, on the fringes of our society perhaps, but as much a part of our community as the pastor or the policeman.

It didn't matter how tough they were on the outside, underneath it all, so many of those men were hurting. Some of them were stuck in their lives, and they needed to feel as if there was something different out there for them; something better. So, they gravitated toward me and told me their stories, and cried real tears for the first time in many years. They were open to all sorts of revelatory ideas, they just couldn't open up in front of any of their peers, little knowing that most of their peers had come to see me too.

But I always felt torn, inauthentic... On the one hand, I had started fasting and spending hours in meditation, thinking about the parallelism of Hinduism and Christianity and how it all worked... And on the other hand, I lived in a world where violence was still the primary language, even if I no longer spoke it myself.

It's true that the lightning strike had changed me in an instant, but it couldn't rewrite my DNA. I wasn't going to be able to escape my genetic inheritance overnight. On some fundamental level, I was still my mother's son, and there was still that fire inside me. Those same violent impulses remained, and I had to get used to the fact that, even if they were buried deep, the violence could sometimes resurface. Years later, when I was doing sculpture and mixed media work, a designer came to me in a bind. He'd promised a downtown Boston bank an elaborate plexiglass installation, but lacked the technical skills to execute it. He asked for my help. I completed the piece, did the installation and waited. Sure enough, he got paid, but he didn't pay me.

I went to his office, determined to handle it like a gentleman. But when he started screaming and following me across the street, something snapped. The next day I returned, pinned him against the wall with my hands around his throat, and said I wouldn't be using legal means to get my money... but that I would be getting my money. He wrote the cheque on the spot. That residue of the old neighborhood, that capacity for violence never fully left me. It would kick in now and then, like a throwback to another time.

Perhaps this was all part of the plan. Changing me outright would have been too easy. What would I have learned about myself and my place in the world if all my violent impulses had been completely expunged?

Years later, I met a man who had been studying with the Dalai Lama, and he told me "When great souls—and great Dalai Lamas—speak for the first time, they act like fools." I realized that it's because they know that life is but a dream and an illusion. They're playing within the dream. I felt that way about Muhammad Ali, the boxer. He interacted with reality on his terms. He didn't take things too seriously; he played at life.

Later still, I took my eldest daughter to see one of the Star Wars films, and it made perfect sense to me how the fool (Yoda) turned out to be the great master. That was so Zen! I have strived all my life to let my stupidity guide me, knowing how the foolish man puts the wise man to shame. So, you'll have to forgive me if I own my idiocy and wear my stupidity with pride!

My experience in the church had opened me up to asking different questions. I was changed, but the world around me stayed the same. In North End, you were supposed to be tough or funny, preferably both. Now I had this other dimension to me that didn't quite fit. It wasn't that I couldn't still be those things, I could still crack jokes with the best of them, still carry myself with the confidence the streets demanded. But something inside me wanted more.

So, I talked about the Bhagavad Gita and Krishna, and fighting without vengeance or violence in your heart, and that kind of thinking resonated strongly with guys like Joe Gorilla, and Vinnie the Animal. They each had their own kind of Samurai code. It was almost an instinctual thing, a way of inuring them against the violence of what they were doing, and from the moral consequences of killing people.

Sal would tell me, "You know, Peter, I hate violence. But whenever I see it, I have to jump in." I knew exactly what he meant. Even after my transformation, I understood that pull. The difference was, now I could see it for what it was: a chain linking us to old patterns, old ways of being. But it took me many more years to stop fighting my craziness and my madness, and learn to accept it as an unavoidable part of me.

The lightning strike didn't just purge the violence from me, it opened my eyes to a different way of seeing the world. The small kindnesses I started seeing all around me seemed like miracles now. It was as if I'd been color-blind before, and suddenly could see the full spectrum of human interaction.

CHAPTER 6

<u>Running with the Wolf</u>

"I was about 17 years old when I stopped a murder in progress. They say, 'no good deed goes unpunished...' and sure enough, about a week later, the would-be killer came after me."

There was a small park up a hill in the Hull Street area in the North End. We called it Slide Park. You could see all of Charlestown from up there on the hill. It was a historic site, an old colonial base called Cops Hill Terrace. It looked like a granite fortress.

I could hear them before I could see them: a circle of guys, baying for blood. I wasn't afraid of whatever it was, although I probably should have been. I made my way up the hill to the park, and when I got close enough, I saw a familiar enough sight. A group of 'tough' guys with one victim, caught like a rat in the centre of the circle. And there lording it over him was Mendez.

Mendez had a big reputation. He was known for his outrageous, unpredictable violence. But above all, Mendez was a bully, and would more than likely pick on the easiest targets. He had this poor Irish kid, Michael, upside down, and he was pounding his head into the pavement. I knew Michael, he was a waiter in a restaurant belonging to my sister and brother-in-law. I'd done a bit of work in there myself and I'd seen Michael around. He didn't have any gang affiliations; he'd probably just been in the wrong place at the wrong time. Maybe he'd caught Mendez's eye and not given due deference, or he'd blanked him altogether. Who knew? In any case, the punishment was the same. And poor Michael was the very definition of an easy target.

Even if I hadn't known Michael, I'd still have done what I did. In my innocence, I just responded to an obvious injustice. Without even thinking, I broke through the crowd and got nose to nose with Mendez—which was just patently unwise, because the guy was scary—and I simply said, "Stop." I already knew I was a dead man.

In that moment, the cacophony died away. Mendez let Michael fall to the ground, where he hunched, fetal. Mendez looked at me. The surprise on his face that anyone as insignificant as me would have the balls to tell him what to do was quickly overtaken by rage. I wasn't afraid of what was coming, and I wasn't about to shirk a fight. Just because I didn't seek violence anymore, it didn't mean I wasn't going to defend myself.

But then, a sound drifted up the hill; it was the unmistakable sound of police sirens, getting closer. It was a beautiful sound. The moment felt as if it had been perfectly choreographed. Everybody ran. Even Mendez. I stayed with the kid, hunched and silent, but he knew I was there, and he knew he was safe. And then, at the last moment, I made my getaway, and the cops arrived and took Michael off to get treated.

About a week later, I was at the corner of Salem and Charter Street, and there he was again—Mendez with his gang—looking for all the world like he'd been waiting for me to show up. I could see him mouthing "You fucking asshole," and he sprang for me. It was as if he'd been on-hold all week, just waiting to pick up where he left off with the job of disconnecting my head from my body.

The cops weren't coming to my assistance this time, but I had something even better... My friend, Lobo. Everyone knew: you don't mess with Lobo! Everyone knew he was a boxer, they probably didn't know he had another, deadlier secret...

Lobo was about half the size of Mendez, but his hands were enormous. In boxing gloves, they looked superhuman. And Lobo got between us and calm as you like, said, "You don't touch him. Ever." That was all it took.

*

I first met Lobo at the gym. I hadn't ever excelled at anything in my time there, but I was a keen boxer, and then, when I was about fourteen, I discovered I had a peculiar strength; my pulling muscles were extraordinarily powerful. While I couldn't bench press much, I could lie on my back and pull over 300 pounds from the floor.

It marked me out as an oddity, I was the kid who could pull incredible weight but wasn't a typical muscle-bound tough guy, and it only added to my mystique. The older guys would gather around the bench to watch me manage tremendous pulls. It was like I had this hidden strength that only emerged in specific circumstances, which made people wonder what else I might be capable of.

I caught the attention of Lobo, but we all called him 'the Wolf'. He looked very much like Sammy the Bull Gravano, except that Lobo had jet black hair. Lobo took me under his wing. He'd watch me work out, and started teaching me about boxing, always telling me to keep my hands up, showing me the techniques. Lobo was about 20-years older than me, and he was a tough guy who came from a tough family. I felt as if he must have emerged fully formed and ready for the streets. Some of those hard men in North End used to play at being tough, they reveled in putting on a bit of a tough guy act, and throwing their weight around. Not Lobo. He just had a quiet aura of innate toughness about him. A presence. He had a particular command of his environment that I've never seen else anyone possess; a way of owning the space he was in.

I knew Lobo had boxed professionally, and I'd seen him sparring a few times. His giant hands could deliver devastating power in the ring, but they could also convey tenderness when he embraced you. He understood nuance in a world that usually dealt only in extremes. Those same hands would grip my shoulders with genuine affection when we met, would pull me into those bear-hug embraces that expressed everything words couldn't say. He moved through the streets of the North End like a force of nature, not threatening exactly, but impossible to ignore. Everyone knew you didn't mess with Lobo.

As our bond grew, Lobo confided in me, but it took a little while before I learned the whole truth about him. One day, visibly upset, he came to see me, and told me how he'd had to kill a man just hours before. I shood have seen it coming: my mentor and protector was a Mafia guy. A hitman.

It didn't change anything between us. The fact of his being a hitman was almost secondary to who he really was. Yes, he had killed people—and I know that saying that so matter-of-factly seems brazenly reductive—but I came to understand that he did it without the same theatrical cruelty of some of the other tough guys. There was no swagger to it, no bragging. He carried the consequences of his actions like a cross he had to bear. When he told me how he had once had to kill three men in one afternoon, it wasn't a boast, it was more like a confession.

Most of the tough guys in North End could only play at being menacing, and loved throwing their weight around, but not Lobo. His quiet aura of assured toughness was something else entirely. Lobo operated to his own innate code of ethics, and that was his way of shielding himself against the violence of what he had to do, and helped him deal with the moral consequences of killing people.

Lobo didn't need to prove anything to anyone. There was no bravado, no showing off. His protection of me came from a place of genuine care, even as his violence came from a place of necessity. It was as if he understood something fundamental about the balance between these forces, something that most of the other tough guys in the neighborhood never quite grasped.

You could see that there was something else about him, something that made him unique among the tough guys. In a world where violence was the primary language, Lobo spoke in deeper truths. He understood things that very few others could grasp, about loyalty, about protection, about the weight of the lives we were living.

When Lobo opened up to me about some of the things he'd done, they were always very tender moments. That may sound strange to you, but that's because it's hard to impose a conventional ethical framework on a world where the rules are so different, where everyone you meet understands the particular laws of the street. I was never going to condemn Lobo. You could almost say that he was simply following his dharma, his path. And his guilt at what he'd had to do, and what he continued to do when called upon, was palpable. I could see how much it cut him up inside. He never once showed that he relished any part of his job, or took any glory in it.

Lobo knew me before and after the lightning strike, and his presence in my life remained constant. He seemed to accept the change in me without question. Maybe he recognized in my change something he wished for himself: a way out of the patterns that held us all. While I was learning to navigate between my transformed inner state and the violent world around me, he showed me it was possible to contain contradictions. He had learned to accept what he was, and what he had to do, while remaining open to the possibility of something more. In his own way, he was as transformed as I was, not by lightning, but by his understanding of duty and consequence.

The change in me helped me see more clearly how men like Lobo carried their burdens. Most of them weren't just tough guys who killed people, they were men trapped by upbringing and lack of opportunity. Like Sal said, he couldn't help jumping into violence, no matter how much he hated it. Lobo was just the same way. He did what he had to do, and accepted the mantle of duty and consequence that came with it.

In those days, if you showed tenderness or questioned the life you were living, you risked being seen as weak. But Lobo's reputation was so solid that he could afford to show his humanity. He could hug me in the street, kiss me on the cheeks and on the lips, like a proper Italian should, and nobody would dare suggest it made him soft. His strength came from somewhere deeper than mere violence. He carried a kind of innate wisdom with him that matched his strength.

It didn't matter if I didn't see Lobo for weeks, months, or years. The bond between us could never be broken. When I was dating Christy, who later became my wife, we walked down to North End, and it was Christy who spotted him further up the street. She could tell there was something about him, just by his aura; just by the way he moved through the space. She could see it writ large in every fiber of his being. She said, "Is that a hitman?" I hissed back, "Yes, but don't say it too loud!" Then, the next thing she knew, he quickened his pace towards us, took me in his giant hands, and we were hugging and kissing like blood brothers. That's the way the Italians do it.

Decades later, at my sister's funeral service, and long after he had died, I talked to Lobo's sister about the early days of our friendship, and of how he'd come to my aid against Mendez. She told me, "You have no idea how many more people have told me stories just like that, and told me how he saved their lives." He was much missed by our entire community. And he was, in many ways the ultimate exemplar of a person who truly understood what it meant to live in North End. Someone who understood both worlds: the violence of the streets and the possibility of striving for something better.

Looking back now, I can see how Lobo was both an anchor to my past and a bridge to my future. He kept me safe in the old world while I was discovering the new one. His protection gave me the space to explore who I was becoming, even as his example showed me that nothing was ever as simple as it seemed.

Even with Lobo's protective presence, I knew I couldn't stay in the North End forever. Perhaps some vestige of the force that had drawn me into that church was pulling me toward something else. The streets had taught me everything they could. It was time for me to learn some new lessons...

PART II

FOLLOWING MY DHARMA

CHAPTER 7

The Song and the Dance

By my late teens, most of my peers were heading off to college, and I found myself looking towards a different kind of future. I had no idea quite what that future was going to look like, I simply knew that it wasn't going to be defined by the expectations of anyone else, not my mother, nor the mafia men, nor my former partners in crime in the Invaders. As I leaned further into Eastern philosophy, so I leaned towards the freedom that comes of simply existing, of drifting like a boat, wherever the breeze took me.

I spent more time with friends whose minds were being opened to possibilities, not closed to the dull certainties of lives and a future predefined by their social standing or academic achievements. Leaving behind some of the "gorillas" in the North End gave me a new perspective. It felt like a wonderful period of growth for me. I remember being increasingly drawn to choral work, and feeling as though I was surrounded by something ethereal. I felt as if I was experiencing a kind of personal renaissance. I was walking the same streets, but travelling on a gentler incline, exploring new ways of thinking.

Music had always been there, waiting for me to find my way to it. Growing up, our house, for all its chaos, had manifested its own kind of harmony. As well as my mother's sometimes spectacular displays of violence, there was beautiful food, cooked with passion, and there was beautiful music. Our Caruso records contained some of the most beautiful music of all. There aren't many six- or seven-year-olds that try and sing along with an Italian tenor, but somehow, I shaped my voice to mirror his.

Apart from appreciating Caruso—he was Italian, after all—my mother didn't exhibit any great musical appreciation or talent. In fact, I think my creativity might have skipped a generation. My father said my grandfather from Calabria had an organ in his house, a piano, and mandolins. He knew all the operas. But it was my uncle, Adgatullo—a well-regarded first violinist who actually owned a Stradivarius—who fostered my interest in singing. His daughter (my father's niece) had studied music for a while, and it broke his heart when she didn't go into music. So, he loved the fact that his nephew had a passion for opera.

If you were going to study singing in Boston at that time, there really was only one place to go: Boston University School of Music[11]. And there was only one teacher that everyone wanted to see...

When the great New York diva Brenda Larson lost her voice through overuse, they directed her to Boston University, saying there was only one guy that was going to help her, and that was David Blair McClosky[12]. He stopped her singing for an entire year, but when she got her voice back, she got her *real* voice back. My uncle was teaching her solfège, and he introduced me to them both. He had already arranged that I should audition for a place studying under McClosky, and when the opportunity came, I must have seemed ridiculous: this streetwise Italian kid trying to sound like Enrico Caruso. At the time, I didn't quite understand the scale of who I was meeting. McClosky was world-renowned. He'd helped the Kennedy brothers with their speaking voices, taught countless opera singers, and years later, when I'd mention McClosky's name to people in the music world, they'd practically cross themselves in reverence. He must have heard something in my voice that day because he decided to take me under his wing. Most people only got to study with students of students of students - the great-grandchildren of the original technique. But I got

---

[11] The Boston University School of Music in the 1960s was undergoing significant changes, integrating traditional classical training with emerging contemporary techniques. The school's connection to the Boston Symphony Orchestra made it a major center for vocal training.

[12] David Blair McClosky (1902-1988) revolutionized vocal pedagogy through his emphasis on relaxation techniques. His method, which became known as the McClosky Technique, was adopted by major music schools worldwide.

to study with the master himself.

Sure enough, the first thing McClosky told me was: Stop singing. He explained that there was a real voice and a false voice, and the real voice could only emerge when the body was completely relaxed. I had to learn to let my whole face relax, all the facial muscles, tongue muscles, throat muscles, and then, and only then, was I allowed to do some light vocalizations.

Letting go of the false voice—the one shaped by ego and the need to sound a certain way—was like peeling away layers of myself. Knowingly or not, McClosky was teaching me to drop the ego, to strip away who I thought I should sound like, so that I could discover who I actually was, without my ego calling the shots. As my mentor and guru, I had to trust in McClosky to lead me to enlightenment with my voice.

I couldn't believe that I could ever sound like a Pavarotti or a Caruso or that I'd ever be able to fill a room without a microphone. I had no inkling that my voice could ever get so strong. He simply said, "Look, it's going to happen," as if it was the most natural thing in the world. "But you've got to remember to keep relaxed. And then we're going to find out what you sound like... what you *really* sound like."

When I started vocalizing again, my real voice was so faint, so delicate, that it barely registered. It was humbling, almost like a spiritual awakening. He assured me that if I trusted the process, then the strength would come. McClosky believed deeply in the relationship between the diaphragm and the voice, and I took that as a kind of spiritual guidance. He'd had many thousands of students over the decades, but told me, entre nous, that I was the only one who grasped the concept of relaxation so quickly. (I felt I'd been practicing that relaxation since I sat in the attic watching the sun travel across the room.)

He saw that I truly understood that relationship between the diaphragm and the voice. The diaphragm is a muscle that most people haven't developed, but boy, do you develop it when you sing! Normally, it's seen as two separate aspects of the whole, but I saw that when you are 100% relaxed, the diaphragm will naturally kick-in to support the voice. Now, when I'm talking to people and they say

"You're 80 years old? You don't sound like you're 80 years old!" But even McClosky was still cutting records with Columbia at the age of 80. He was a baritone with a beautiful voice. And that was a sure sign that a properly trained voice would last.

McClosky's training gave me the tools to understand not just my voice but my presence in the world. Singing wasn't just about sound; it was about movement, expression, and energy. I sang in an opera at Boston University, did some solo performances and sang in church. But I got bored easily. McClosky once asked me did I want to sing or not? In retrospect, I can see how that was the wrong question. The better question was: "Did I want to *perform* or not?" Because I did not want to sing professionally, but to this day, I have never stopped performing!

Wherever life took me after that, I realized that I was still singing the song, and dancing the dance. From negotiating with De Beers in London or pitching ideas to ICT in Michigan, my voice and my performative style were my tools of persuasion. McClosky didn't just coach my voice, he changed the way I moved through space.

I had always noticed how, when Lobo moved, every element of every motion seemed to come so intuitively, without falseness or artifice. As if his very essence expressed itself in each and every stride. I don't know if he had been born with that confidence or if he grew into it, but it was one of the things I most admired about him. His movements were so truthful and so revealing of who he was. McClosky helped me to express myself more openly and authentically. It made it easier for me to move between my disparate worlds, one day discussing vocal technique at Boston University, another day, interacting with Mafia men on the streets, and the next, in deep contemplation of the mysteries of life and spirituality.

McClosky also changed the way I listened, helping me to listen beyond what people said to intuit what they really wanted to say. The sensitivity I developed through training—the ability to hear subtle shifts in tone and rhythm—allowed me to read people, to understand what they weren't saying as much as what they were. It was like dancing with words, moving through time and space with purpose.

I am reminded of an Irish friend, Russell Britt, who could walk into a bank, sit himself down in front of the most senior manager and get whatever he wanted, without ever having to raise his voice or threaten anyone. Later in life Russell persuaded me to go into a partnership with him in a carpentry business. He had the gift of the blarney as the Irish would say. In no time, they'd be saying, "Russ, we're going to give you a million dollars for this project." And then he'd say, "Well, you might just as well throw in another million." And if they tried to tell him that would be ridiculous, he'd say, "Look, it's just as ridiculous for you to give me a million as two million." So they'd end up giving him whatever he asked for. Some people have a gift. They know how their whole body commands attention, and they know how to present themselves with such authority that no one can deny them.

The influence of my voice training has lingered. I've found myself using it unconsciously, like when I host guests at our Airbnb. It's not just the words I say, but how I say them, the pacing, the energy, the performance. One of our guests, Christian from Scotland, taught a course combining business and theater, and I told him, "You've got it. That's brilliant!" Life is theater, after all, and knowing how to perform makes all the difference.

I was great friends with a guy from Madeira called Gil DeJesus. Gil had been a professional bassoonist, but his life changed one day when he met Andrés Segovia, the legendary classical guitarist[13]. He told me he sat in Segovia's hotel room for 30 or 45 minutes in complete silence. Segovia didn't say a word, but somehow, just being in that room with the great guitarist transformed him. After that meeting, he never picked up the bassoon again. He became a classical guitarist, purely through the influence of Segovia's presence.

---

[13] Andrés Segovia (1893-1987) transformed the classical guitar from a folk instrument into one worthy of concert halls. Born in Linares, Spain, he began playing guitar at age four and, despite his parents' opposition to his musical pursuits, went on to revolutionize the instrument's technique and repertoire. Segovia's impact on classical music extended far beyond his technical innovations - he possessed what many described as an almost mystical presence that profoundly affected those around him.

That was typical of Segovia's ability to inspire through "silent teaching." He believed that music transcended verbal instruction, and that true artistry had to be channeled via deeper, more intuitive means. To him the guitar was a medium for expressing the soul's truth. I couldn't help but be reminded of McClosky's teachings. Both artists shared the same belief in the mysterious ineffable power of music that goes beyond human classification. The playwright Federico García Lorca called this mysterious power "duende," and it is widely embraced in flamenco culture where the dancer's ability to transmit heartfelt emotion and reveal inner truth without words or even music, but rather, through their mere presence, really resonated with me.

One night, I was out drinking beer at the famous European Restaurant in the North End, with Gil and our friend Nino, who played flamenco. The flamenco style is so raw, emotive, and improvisational—closer to jazz or blues in its spirit. Flamenco, like those genres, is about motion, emotion, and freedom. It's not structured the way Segovia's style was. It's like asking a ballerina to suddenly dance modern jazz, it's a completely different world. We were debating whether Segovia, with his towering intellect and refined technique, could ever play flamenco like the great Spanish flamenco guitarist, Sabicas[14]. A fat Hawaiian guitarist that none of us particularly liked muscled into the conversation. He was adamant that Segovia could master flamenco, but the three of us were equally convinced that he couldn't. "Your head's up your ass!" we said. The Hawaiian guitarist just happened to be sitting across from me, and as we argued, a piece of pizza went down the wrong way. I had a mouthful of beer, and before I knew it, I'd sprayed the unhappy (and unloved) guitarist with beer. It was completely unintentional, of course, but it became the crowning absurdity of the evening.

McClosky's training gave me the foundation to express myself, whether in business, storytelling, or even just casual conversation. The techniques he taught me became second nature, woven into the fabric of who I am. And even though I never pursued a career in singing, I've never stopped performing. And that same streak of

---

[14] Sabicas (16 March 1912 – 14 April 1990) was a Spanish flamenco guitarist of Romani origin.

53

creativity has surfaced in all of my children, particularly in my youngest daughter, Ariel.

Going way beyond music, McClosky showed me that finding your true voice means first learning to be still, to let go of who you think you should be. Whether I was singing opera or making deals, that lesson stayed with me. The voice, like life itself, works best when you stop forcing it, and you let it flow naturally. It was a lesson that resonated throughout my life.

CHAPTER 8

Finding My Own Way

"No guides, no roadmaps. You'll have to figure it all out yourself."

As a very young teen, even before my time with McClosky, I'd gone to the local Franciscan monastery in search of some answers, or at least some sense of connection with other seekers of deeper spiritual truth. One of their Order listened as I told him about all my thinking on theology, religion, and life's mysteries. After a while, he said he had something for me and appeared to glide off in his floor-length habit. When he returned, he presented me with a book called *Seeds of Contemplation*, written by Thomas Merton. That was my first exposure to the great theologian.

Merton had been a Trappist monk for 26 years. But far from being a by-the-book Catholic, he was a bit of a trailblazer. We think of him now as the first Catholic mystic, and he was responsible for bringing more Eastern thought—including elements of Buddhism, and ideas around harnessing the breath—into Christianity.[15] What made Merton's ideas particularly difficult for the Catholic orthodoxy to grapple with was his ability to articulate these connections in a way that made ancient wisdom accessible to modern practitioners. (Almost as if he drew the veil away from the old, arcane wisdom that had been the exclusive province of upper echelons of clergy.) He drew parallels between Zen breathing meditation and the Christian contemplative tradition, suggesting that mindful breathing could deepen one's experience of Christ's presence.

---

[15] Thomas Merton (1915-1968) was instrumental in opening dialogue between Eastern and Western spiritual traditions. His 1968 meetings with the Dalai Lama marked a turning point in Buddhist-Christian relations.

He also did more than any man to popularize the religious life. In the aftermath of World War II, there was a greater influx of men into monasteries and women into convents, all of them had been traumatized by the atrocities, and all were searching for something deeper and more profound. Merton was instrumental in that. At a time when people wanted to break down barriers, his pursuit of spiritual truth seemed like it transcended some of the frontiers between the world religions.

I devoured *Seeds of Contemplation* and started to apply Merton's thinking to my life straightaway. He said you have to give up all your desires, and all your ambitions, and that made sense to me. I felt as if the only reason I had any ambitions was because I was expected to have ambitions. But a life of ambition seemed to me to be predicated on procuring more money to amass more things, and more status, and that didn't interest me in the slightest.

I had spent so long thinking that perhaps I should try and cultivate some ambitions because I felt so isolated and alone on my path. (In truth, I wasn't very good at it; I think pursuing ambition just gave me a bad case of spiritual indigestion, and so I always went back to ascetism in the end.) But Merton made it clear that those ambitions were just the root of illusion. And so, I let go of my ambitions. It wasn't that difficult when I'd already spent so much of my energy trying to escape the idea that I should be judged according to the role I took in life. The absence of worldly desire was startling, the relief was instantaneous.

A perfect peace came over me. I hardly knew what it was at first. I sat, very still, in the attic room, and slipped out of the shackles of conventional thinking. I stopped thinking of who and what I had to become and let my ego take a back seat. As Merton taught, it is only when you stop trying to be someone you don't want to be, and when you eschew the idea of religious and social conformity, that things magically align and convey inner peace.

There was nothing abstract about Merton's teachings, they all made practical sense to me. The link between emptying my mind and my very soul of the sorts of routine desires that plagued the rest of the world was clear. And the more I found out about the man, the more I loved him. It was his very human frailties – his flaws, if you like – that made him such a compellingly relatable figure.

Merton's teachings helped me to pick apart this idea that perfection had anything to do with enlightened thinking. What use is a perfect system in an imperfect world? Peter, the imperfect disciple, was made the first head of the Catholic church after all. And it seemed to me as if there should be a loosening of the perception of what constituted good Catholicism. I didn't want to lead a strict ascetic life, I wanted to lead a life that was full of colour. And I felt as if that kind of existence was much more likely to lead me towards something transformative.

Inspired by Merton's own path, and the possibilities of embracing elements of all three religions, I stayed with the Trappist monks for a few weeks at a time, I wondered if I should join them to pursue my journey into deeper spirituality. I met Father Mark, who wasn't just a Catholic monk, he was a medical doctor too. He indulged me with his time and patience, as he listened to my thoughts, answered my questions, and most importantly, gave me the sense that my spiritual quest was worthwhile.

Father Mark told me that I was wise beyond my years. My precociousness made me seem like a prodigy to him. But in my mind, it was almost as if I was simply picking up from where I had left off in some other lifetime. Years later, when I went back for a visit after I'd got married and had a child, Father Mark said to me, "Peter, the reason why we kept on raising the age limit when you got old enough to join us is because we knew you were going to have a problem with women." He wasn't wrong.

Merton talked about how terrifying the monastic life can be because you lose all the guideposts—the trees and roads that tell you which way to go. You are absolutely alone in your monastic journey. It's a state where you question everything: *Can I find God in this direction? Am I following the right path?* You even question yourself. But somehow, he said, if you persevere, then intuition guides you to stay and to find the resolve to commit yourself to your devotions. And that's where the beauty lies...

I experienced that terror and that beauty during my time in the monasteries. It was the rigidity of structure that frightened me most, the sense that you could achieve enlightenment or some form of communion with the Divine, but only if you used the right Catholic / Hindu / Buddhist rulebook. I sought a more product-agnostic approach. But in matters of organised religion, you're encouraged to sing from the same hymn sheet. (Which is a shame when the other teams have some pretty nice songs too.)

I saw the beauty of absolute surrender to monastic life too. There was something inspiring in the complete absence of worldly ambition that Merton talked about, and in the silence. I don't mean that you can only find that kind of silence in a monastery, but it's a lot easier to commit to the silence and really subject yourself to it in a place where there are no other distractions. But it really does require that you subject yourself to it. That's' when you find out if silence is a blessing or a curse; it takes a lot of mental strength to live with yourself, in silence, 24-hours a day.

I could see how some people were so perfectly, serenely, adapted to their monastic life, and those people shone out to me like latter-day prophets. I remember this one old monk; he seemed to radiate light. His eyes were luminous, his whole being vibrated as if he had a halo. The other monks told me how he spent his days: reading obituaries and praying for the deceased. That was his life's work, and you could feel the goodness in him. More than that, it seemed to me that he was following his dharma / his true path.

But the rigidity of inviolable dogma was not for me. And nor was salvation by rote orthodoxy. I know that some people need the reassurance of structure, and they should embrace that. But for others, like me, the path needs to be more fluid.

I used to be able to tell which art school someone went to just by the structure of their paintings. For example, Boston University alumni's work was very structured, but the Museum School's alumni had no structure at all. It was fascinating to see how the lack of structure could produce either chaos or brilliance. With no weight of preconceived ideas, you can accelerate quickly—if you know where you're going. It's like studying concert piano and then getting up on stage, letting go of everything, and just playing. That's what my spiritual journey has been like - learning all the rules and structures, then learning when to let them go.

Some Buddhist monasteries have far less structure than the monasteries I spent time in, and I've read that those places can produce either the greatest saints or the greatest sinners. Absolute freedom of spirit can lead to incredible growth, but it can also lead to terrible choices if you're misled. Walking that line is dangerous and challenging.

My early experiences in the monasteries taught me both the value of discipline and the importance of finding my own way. When I combined elements of prayer, meditation, and mindful breathing, it really didn't matter to me which strand of theology I used to tap into the Divine, it's the intent that counts. There is a wonderful Hindu story that illustrates this:

God sent an angel down to earth to look for devout people. Sure enough, the angel found lots of devout people. In his first trip, he found a guru who knew the Bhagavad Gita backwards and forwards, and another guru who couldn't stop praying and praising God, but when the angel went back to report to God, he was disappointed by His response. God said, "I don't know these people." The angel couldn't understand how God didn't know such devout people. God said, "Who else is there?"

So, the angel went back and found many more holy people and told God about them. Again, God said, "But I don't know these people." The angel kept looking. Among all the holy people, he saw a man on the hill, who was trying to build a fence. But the man was so drunk that he kept hitting his hand with his hammer, and cursing every time he did it. The angel made sure he remembered the names of all the holy people he'd seen, as well as the name of the man on the hill. He told God of all the holy people, and God was unimpressed. "Was there no one else?" he asked.

"Well, there was one other man," the angel ventured. He told God about the man on the hill, hardly expecting God to acknowledge him. But God said, "Oh yeah, that's Harry. I know him very well. Harry loves me."

God told the angel to go back to Harry, and mention that he had sent him. When the angel announced himself to Harry, the man transformed and entered into a Divine dance with the angel; another level of consciousness. The angel began to understand. God told him. "The prayers are nice, but all I really want is love. I can feel Harry's passion when he speaks to me. I can feel his love."

That story resonated deeply with my own experience of spirituality, both inside and outside the monastery walls. Throughout my life there have been times when I've lived a quasi-monastic lifestyle. I'd go into isolation to pray, meditate, and fast. I wouldn't see anyone—especially not women—and that was always a struggle. I never felt as if I had all the answers; I was just trying to figure things out for myself. And it seemed to me that God must have read Thomas Merton's book, and as if to prove its veracity, decided that I should have to stumble around in the dark. I could picture God looking upon me and saying, "I'm going to give you nothing. No guides, no roadmaps. You'll have to figure it all out yourself."

Maybe that's a good thing. It's all too easy to get stuck on the idea of a set way of doing things. That's why in Buddhism, they say, "If you see Buddha, kill Buddha." Buddha shouldn't be a concept. You have to be totally free. That's also why, in Islam, there are no images of God—it's about maintaining total freedom from attachment. But as Merton said, that freedom can be terrifying too. Without those guideposts, without those familiar markers of progress, how do you know if you're moving in the right direction?

I think the answer is that you're not supposed to know. Surely, that terrifying freedom is where real growth happens. It's like those coal ovens in the old restaurants that needed constant attention but made the best pizza. Maybe our spiritual lives need that same kind of engagement. It's not just about following a recipe, but feeling our way through, adjusting as we go, trusting our instincts while staying alert to the results.

Perhaps we're supposed to accumulate the understanding over several lifetimes? Maybe in a few hundred years, I'll have learned enough through successive lifetimes, but for now, the lesson is to stumble through this life, relying on my intuition and experience.

Practicing stupidity like a wise man who knows he knows nothing. Living life with a cigar in hand, a song in my heart, and a smile on my lips.

CHAPTER 9

Escape From Vietnam

"Sometimes the clearest certainty comes without a plan"

I was drafted towards the end of the decade and was expected—if not outright required—to go to Vietnam. I knew immediately that I couldn't go. It wasn't just that I was afraid of the violence, or of the prospect of jungle war; growing up in North End, I'd obviously been exposed to more than my share of violence. It just didn't make sense to me. I had no quarrel with those people. Why would I go fight in a war that had nothing to do with me?[16]

More than that, it would have been an uncomfortable scenario for someone who had been converted to the pursuit of peace in my miraculous transfiguration in St. Stephen's... but I didn't think that would have been a valid, government-mandated reason for getting out of military service!

I went for the physical, hoping that they'd uncover some reason why I was unfit for service. But they said I was in good shape, strong, and fit for duty. There wasn't long to wait between being approved and getting a date of departure, and sure enough, I received word that I should report to the drafting office in just a few days. (It doesn't pay to keep new recruits waiting too long, trigger fingers twitching uncomfortably.)

With the day of departure at hand, the family shut down the restaurant, and the cooks stayed late to prepare a farewell feast for me. The restaurant was packed with friends and family saying

---

[16] The Boston area was a center of draft resistance during the Vietnam War. Notable events included the turning in of draft cards at Arlington Street Church in October 1967, with participants including Howard Zinn and Noam Chomsky.

goodbye, assuming I was heading off to the jungles of Vietnam, and wondering perhaps, if they'd ever see me again.

Even at that late stage, I was resolute in my belief that I wasn't going, I just didn't have a workable plan for how I was going to get out of it, and time was running out. My brother-in-law, who was one of the co-owners of the restaurant, was suspicious. "You're much too happy for someone who's about to go to war," he said. I suppressed a smile. The ineffable sense that somehow, I was going to be protected was growing in me.

The official plan was that my father and my brother-in-law would pick me up early in the morning and drive me to the Customs House in Boston. But my own plan was to leave before they got to me. I wasn't planning on disappearing and never returning, I just had no intention of being sent to war. It was a pretty rudimentary plan, and it might have been executed effectively if I hadn't been quite so good at sleeping through my alarm. Sure enough, I overslept and woke to the sound of them downstairs waiting for me.

There was nothing for it, but to pack for departure, and go along with it in the faint hope of some sort of miracle or Divine intervention. (But I reasoned that I'd probably used up my allocation of revelatory experiences and Divine interventions for one lifetime.) Resigned, I packed my bag and got into the back of the car. I can only remember thinking, quite absurdly, about where I was going to find good espresso or pizza in the jungle.

We arrived at the Customs House, and I suggested they wait in the car while I went to see what was happening inside. It was a cavernous building, with doors on all four sides. I walked in, passed straight through, exited on the opposite side, and just kept on walking. When I got to the park beyond, I settled myself down, with no idea of a plan, or a strategy, sat on the grass, and fed the birds and squirrels. In the midst of all the drama of absconding from my military service, I felt about as content as one could feel, surrounded by nature, innocently engaged in my little communions with the animals.

I guessed that my father and my brother-in-law would have naturally assumed that I'd been successfully inducted, and returned to the North End. I had nowhere else to go, and no means of getting there anyway. So, after enough time had passed—and I assumed I was safe from being rounded up and bundled in with all the other new recruits—I started to make my way home, walking the long miles, not quite knowing what I was going to do when I got there.

For all its size—60,000 people in one square mile—the North End was really like a big village, and word soon got around that I was back. As returns of prodigal sons go, mine was one of the least wondrous. Of course, people were shocked to see me. "What the fuck are you doing here? Aren't you supposed to be fighting the Viet Cong?" they asked.

I could cope with all of that, but I thought my father was going to strangle me for leaving without a word, never mind running away from the war. But when he saw me, he burst out laughing. Maybe there was something in my impudent refusal to accede to authority that impressed him more than my meekly going along with my call up could ever have done.

I wasn't out of the jungle yet though. The US Army wasn't going to let me go that easily. So my father went to the head of the draft board, a woman named Mary Lynn, to request a psychiatric evaluation, hoping it would prove my unsuitability for service. I knew I'd had my one and only Bonafide miracle, but the little miracles kept on coming... It transpired that Mary's own nephew had resisted his draft, and she empathized with my plight.

For six months, I was an outpatient at Mass Mental Hospital, where I met with countless psychiatrists. I went through endless evaluations, including the Rorschach test. I'd describe what I saw in the inkblots, and I remember one psychiatrist incredulously asking, "You see what?!" I stood by my answers. In our final meeting, all the psychiatrists gathered with the head doctor. They suggested I should claim to be a Quaker, or a conscientious objector, but I refused. "No," I said, "I'm none of those things. I'm just not going. This conflict has nothing to do with me."

They wrote a letter to the army explaining my situation, hoping it would keep me out of jail. During the meeting, the head psychiatrist told my father, "We can't find anything wrong with your son..." My father felt that if the psychiatrist passed me as 'normal' then the army would certainly put me in jail, so the psychiatrist wrote a letter explaining that I was definitely not military material. Then the psychiatrist asked if my father would like to come in for some treatment. My father nearly fell out of his chair. "You think my son's normal and I'm the crazy one?!" To reassure him the psychiatrist said, "I can see this whole issue is really upsetting you." My father was a sensitive soul, but we both left without any further psychiatric intervention.

A few weeks later, the army sent me a letter asking me to see their psychiatrists. I ignored it. Then they sent a second letter. I ignored that too. A third letter followed, and I ignored that as well. Eventually, I received a notice saying I was deferred for one year with a one-year classification. After that, I never heard from them again.

Buoyed by my freedom, I lived life to the full... I even got married!

My first wife was Donna, and I stole her from one of the wiseguys in the North End. At the time, I was hanging out with the older guys on Hanover Street.[17] In the eyes of those older guys, I was still just a kid, but after St. Stephen's I was widely regarded as wise beyond my years. One of the guys in that circle, known as El Cid[18], had a big Harley, and one summer night, around one or two in the morning, he came down the street with a beautiful redhead on the back of the bike. While he wasn't looking, I caught her eye, and slipped her my phone number. We started seeing each other, and, of course, he found out.

One night, I heard a woman's voice shouting from ground level,

---

[17] The main artery of Boston's North End, Hannover Street has been the heart of the city's Italian-American community since the late 19th century. In the 1960s and early 1970s, the street maintained its distinctive character as a blend of legitimate businesses, social clubs, and less official enterprises. Local folklore held that the real business of the neighborhood happened after midnight, when the tourists and casual visitors had gone home.

[18] The nickname "El Cid" references the legendary Spanish military leader and folk hero, Rodrigo Díaz de Vivar (1043-1099), known as El Cid Campeador. Plenty of the mob guys took on nicknames to try and build their cachet and cement their legendary status.

telling me to go and look out the window. From my fourth-floor apartment I could see it was Donna, and standing next to her was El Cid. With the rising moon shining behind him, he looked absolutely enormous. Standing 6'3", he must have weighed at least 275 pounds. He had the most imposing presence of any mafia man I ever met, and I met a few. He had a way of making every little action look casual, as if to impress upon people he really could not give a fuck about the mundanities of life. With the merest twitch of two fingers on his right hand, he beckoned me down to join them, and I complied. Of course I did, what else could I do?

I tried to give Donna a reassuring look, but she barely dared look at me. El Cid gestured for her to get in the back, and motioned me around to the front to sit next to him. He pulled the Cadillac out and we shot off the wrong way down a one-way street. I'd like to say that was indicative of his devil-may-care attitude, but as you'll have learned by now, there was a fierce anarchistic streak running through us all in North End, none of us bothered with those sorts of rules.

Knowing what was to come, I didn't want that journey to come to an end, but before I knew it, we were in the middle of the woods. It seemed as if everything had been planned in advance so that even our route through the trees had been carefully mapped out. He stopped the car, reached down, and pulled out a black suede satchel from under his seat. Very delicately, he started to unfold, and I saw that there was a selection of knives inside. Each knife was beautifully polished, and tapered off to a razor-sharp tip. He made a show of pulling the knives, one-by-one, and examining the immaculate blades in the moonlight that shone through the windshield.

It was almost artistic, like something out of an auteur's gangster film, and El Cid played his part to perfection. As he took each new knife in his hand, he talked me through what it was "This is a skinning knife... This is a deboning knife..." Suddenly, he leant over towards me and stuck one of the knives against my throat. I had a close beard at the time, and he said, "Do you want a shave?"

I'd been in tight spots before, and spent enough time on the streets of North End to know that was not the time to show fear. I had to keep calm, no matter what, so I just said, "No, that's all right. I plan on shaving tomorrow."

He looked me in the eye and said, "Listen, kid. If you see her again, I'm going to kill you. I'm going to kill your family. I'm putting a vendetta on you." That was supposed to be the signal for me to beg for forgiveness, but I wasn't so easily cowed. Even though I knew that one word of repentance from me and a promise to keep my distance would have been enough to appease him, I didn't like making promises that I knew I wasn't going to be able to keep. So, I didn't give him the satisfaction. I held his gaze, and by the time he understood I wasn't going to baulk, he pulled the knife away, put the satchel back under his seat, and pulled the car back onto the road.

Maybe I'd missed that sort of conflict, maybe I'd enjoyed pushing myself out of my comfort zone, or maybe I was just showing the world that no one could tell Peter Catizone what to do... Whatever it was, I can't tell you how much I enjoyed the journey back, knowing that I'd stared him down and lived to tell the tale. The next day, I called Donna and said, "Let's get together."

After that, El Cid was surprisingly nice to me, with the caveat that he kept trying to get me to go out on his boat. It didn't take a big leap of imagination to suppose that if I had stepped foot on that boat, I'd probably never have been seen again. But I think that night in the woods was some form of contractual obligation, something he'd had to be seen to do. He'd tried to rattle me and failed, and as a result, I'd earned his grudging respect. I showed him I had balls—what the Italians call *coglioni*. Plus, my family had some connections of their own with the boss of bosses, a guy named Arigo Selvitella. (When you had disputes that needed sorting out, people would get in line to speak to him at the Florenitine bar, where he held court.) All it would have taken was a word with him, and things would have got sorted out a good deal more messily.

When Donna and I got married, it was in Guarente's Funeral Parlor. The owner, who was also a justice of the peace, conducted the ceremony on the second floor, while someone was being laid out downstairs. It was surreal and hysterical in its way. Oh, and the church next to the funeral parlor? That was St Stephen's, the same church that was struck by lightning.

Apparently, the place is haunted. Much later in life, I had a couple of guests staying with me who were spiritualists, and without knowing the history of the place said they felt as if they were being touched – and it wasn't my wandering hands..

As it turned out, getting married didn't incur the wrath of the infamous El Cid. Sure, we may not have invited him to the wedding, but he didn't give us any more trouble. After a whirlwind few months, I never quite escaped the fear of being ensnared by someone. If not El Cid, then the government...

A few weeks later, I was at a beach in Duxbury with Donna and her friend. We were lying on the sand when an army helicopter hovered above us. I was convinced they'd found me and were finally going to take me away and drop me straight into the jungle (in my bathing suit) to face the Viet Cong. Of course, they were just checking out the two women in bikinis, but my paranoia lingered for years.

Even now, little things like official letters and jury duty notices can trigger that same fear of being caught. Whenever I received a jury duty summons, I'd write "deceased" on it and return it to sender. After a couple of attempts, they stopped sending them.

It's funny, one psychic once told me I'd been imprisoned in a dungeon in England centuries ago. He described me as well-dressed, someone of royal blood or means, who'd had his land and money taken by the establishment. Apparently, I was really pissed off about that! Another psychic said I had been trying to reform the system legally but had been targeted by the powers-that-be. True or not, I do know that when I was in London later, I felt an uneasiness, as though I'd lived through something there. At the same time, it felt like home. It cemented in me the sense that I'd developed a health streak of iconoclasm in my past lives, that had found full voice in the present.

CHAPTER 10

<u>In the Valley of the Wasp</u>

"When you think you're escaping into the wilderness, sometimes you're really coming home to yourself"

Ever since the age of 15, I'd lived without a plan. It went back to Thomas Merton's idea of giving up all ambitions and desires. When you live without goals, you end up wherever life places you. That felt like the right way to live life. You engaged in life without any sense of your future needs; it reminded me of that part of scripture when Christ is resurrected and tells his disciples how to approach missionary work. They ask how long they should stay in a particular house, and Christ replies, "Stay until you leave." That's beautiful advice, really, and it summed up how I lived. I stayed until it was time to leave.

It meant that we were effectively free to go anywhere and do anything we wanted. So, when we saw an advert for people to join a group who wanted volunteers to help them in their effort to rebuild a little piece of history, we were ready for the adventure. There was a grant from the Smithsonian Institute to rebuild a pottery in Jugtown, North Carolina[19]. It got that name because during the colonial period, potters who came from Staffordshire, England settled in that part of North Carolina, drawn by the abundance of clay beds in the soil. In the nineteen twenties an American couple—the Busby's—took over and rebuilt the site. But when they left, the site deteriorated and fell

---

[19] Jugtown Pottery, established in 1917 in Seagrove, North Carolina, was founded by Jacques and Juliana Busbee. The pottery was known for its unique glazes and traditional techniques brought from Staffordshire, England. The Smithsonian's involvement in the 1960s marked a growing national interest in preserving American craft traditions.

into obsolescence.

The grant from the Smithsonian was to rebuild the infrastructure, including the homes and buildings the potters had built, exactly as they had been, using traditional techniques from that period. We went for the interview, and as I had just finished studying a course in ceramics at the Museum of Fine Arts in Boston, I was a good candidate. I'd even built an artistic variant on a kick wheel—a massive thing made of oak. It was so big you had to climb into it. One day, my artists friends Keiko and Perry—who was a talented jewelry sculptor—came over. Perry looked at the kick wheel and said, "Peter, that's not a kick wheel... That's a piece of sculpture." I hadn't realized I was building sculptures until he pointed it out. He said, "It may very well function as a kick wheel, but it looks like something from another world."

Jugtown gave us a diversion from real life; it was like stepping back in time to a simpler age, and there was something in that that really appealed to me. Rejecting modernity and embracing a more ascetic life appealed to my monastic tendencies.

We worked hard at rebuilding the cabins and restoring the kilns to their former glory, living simply, and enjoying the simple pleasure of construction and renovation. The kilns were long, dome-shaped structures with arches, beautifully built and still fit-for-purpose. We dug our own clay out of the ground[20] and would typically process it using a pug mill—a machine that removes inconsistencies and creates a smooth textured clay. In our case, we used a horse-operated pug mill. It was quite the joke. The horse loved Mountain Dew. We had a soda machine in the sales cabin, and I'd grab a Mountain Dew and hold it in front of the horse. The horse was attached to a giant log with spokes, similar to what you'd see in wine-making setups. The clay went into the pug mill, and the horse mixed it up by walking in

---

[20] The clay deposits in the Seagrove area of North Carolina are among the finest in North America, which explains why the original Staffordshire potters chose this location. The clay's unique mineral composition makes it particularly suitable for traditional pottery techniques.

circles. Afterward, as a reward, I'd let the horse drink the Mountain Dew. It was hilarious.

We worked with lead glazes. Yes, they were dangerous but verisimilitude trumps health and safety, right? We were aiming for authenticity in all things. For stoneware, we would climb on top of the kilns while they were firing—what did I say about health and safety?—and throw handfuls of salt inside. The salt would melt over the pottery, creating a glaze.

That whole time was like a dream of heat and toil. Light-headed with lead fumes, it was easy to think that the barriers between our times and the Busby's were that little bit more malleable and ethereal. When our time at Jugtown came to an end, and we had to step out of the past into the present, we didn't know where life would take us next. But that didn't phase us. We were getting used to the idea that life didn't fit to a roadmap, it was a series of unknown adventures, each one waiting to be discovered. And we were about to embark on one of life's greatest adventures...

In 1969, Donna gave birth to our daughter, Sarah. We didn't know where life was going to take the three of us, but we rode the uncertainty and reveled in living life in a state of eternal flux. It was the spirit of the time. In the sixties, we were all rejecting the norms of society, and just going with the flow; winging it. There was an excitement to that. Even when traveling, we'd only ever have a rough map, rarely knowing exactly where we were going.

Maybe it was all tied to some past life when I lived in a tent in Arabia. Or maybe it was all tied up in the hippie ideal of living in the moment. In those days, you didn't do what society expected, you didn't go and join your father's corporation, you took the time to 'find yourself'. You went to live in the woods, or in a tipi and lived a simpler life.

So that's what we did. In the spring of 1969, we moved out of the mundane world of aspiration and desire and made ourselves a home in the woods. It was an old gold and copper mine that belonged to my friend Buddy Sherman. Soon after we arrived, I stopped a logger who was just about to log the 160-acre site illegally, and when they found out, Buddy's family in Chicago made me the legal caretaker. I was like the custodian of the land.

Living in splendid isolation in the Oregon Mountain National Forest with an infant, and my wolf dog, we strived to learn a different way of life.[21] When you travel in hope you don't always get to where you need to be without a bit of help. By the time we were close to the site we'd chosen for our new home, we needed a bit of help to find our way. We stopped at the first building we'd seen for miles, called the Magic Forest Farm. (That name might have given me a clue as to its true nature.) On my way to the door, I passed a big opaque dome, and I could see that there were figures inside, but I couldn't make out any details.

I knocked at the door, and a woman answered, completely nude except for an apron. I'd never seen anything like that in the North End! She was quite a large woman, and everything was out on display. With a big smile on her face, she said, "Hi, my name's Jean, what's your name?" It took me a second or two to remember my name, before I blurted out, "My name's Peter."

She gave me directions up into the mountains, and as I turned to go back to the car, I saw through the opening of the opaque dome. There were seats in a circle all around the perimeter, and there was a gaggle of kids coloring, some women knitting, and they were all completely naked. The Magic Forest Farm was a hippy commune. When I got back to the car, Donna asked, "What happened?" I said, "I'm not quite sure, but it's going to be very interesting!"

Takilma Valley was known by the indigenous Americans as the valley of the wasp.[22] The ground was coarse and riddled with wasp tunnels. It was impossible to walk around—let alone work the land—without getting stung. The plagues of wasps in the summer were of Biblical

---

[21] The Oregon Mountain National Forest in the late 1960s became a focal point of the back-to-land movement. Between 1967-1972, an estimated 100,000 people attempted some form of homesteading in the Pacific Northwest.

[22] The Takilma Valley, named for its indigenous inhabitants, was known to Native Americans as "Valley of the Wasp" due to its unique ground-nesting yellow jacket populations. The Takelma people inhabited the region for over 8,000 years before European settlement.

proportions. My daughter was too young to know better and would hit out at the wasps, and they would sting her for it. I had to pour gasoline in the holes and cover them with a rock, just so we could have any land fit for living on.

There was something quite Biblical about setting off into the wilderness without any sense of how we were going to survive. It wasn't quite like going into exile for forty days and nights, but the symbolism struck me nonetheless. After my stay in the monastery and my work with the wiseguys, my thinking continued to move towards ways of embracing the three strands of Christianity, Hinduism, and metaphysics in my life. That was my holy Trinity, the source of my spiritual yearning. And you might say that I found some of what I was searching for in that remote place...

On my first day, I didn't look for water until I got thirsty. Then, I discovered a particularly wet part of a nearby meadow and climbed the mountain until I found the source. There were three trickles of water coming from three underground springs. Holding onto the side of the mountain with one hand, I made a channel with my other hand, combining the three trickles into one channel of water. At the base of the mountain, I dug a large hole and lined it with rocks, and it provided an endless supply for me and the animals. I was even able to fashion a gravity flow garden on the mountain slope and could supply water to different parts of the garden by moving a few rocks around.

The final tributary carried water to the deep inground bathtub that I built. The sun warmed the water during the day, making it wonderfully inviting by the evening. Each day's dirty water would drain off, and the process would repeat the next day. The three streams of water that I fashioned into one lifegiving stream was a beautiful symbol of my thinking, and it continued to serve me well.

In the summer, I worried that there wouldn't be enough water for us to survive. I had planned to burrow further into the mountain to increase the water flow, but I met an old man who told me that if I tried to dig it out, I'd run the risk of changing its direction and losing it altogether. So, I left it alone. That summer was blisteringly hot. All the water sources dried up in the valley below. But my three trickles of water flowing into one never changed. Forever constant. My Trinity.

CHAPTER 11

Life in the Wilderness

"The simplest existence often yields the most profound truths"

We camped through the summer into Fall, and beyond... We ended up under canvas far longer than we'd ever anticipated. I'd been expecting a friend and his brother to come out and help me build a larger cabin. They certainly had the muscle, they used to beat up Hell's Angels in nightclubs in Laguna Beach. The taller brother, Tony, was about 6'9", and he probably could have taken a felled tree under each arm quite comfortably, but they weren't able to stay. Before they left, Tony asked if he could plant marijuana seeds on my property. I didn't want it to happen, but I wasn't about to say 'no' to Tony. Secretly, I willed them not to grow. Sure enough, not a single seed germinated. He was baffled, but I felt that on an unconscious, spiritual level I must have had something to do with it. I didn't want them to take seed, and they didn't. Some things just weren't meant to take root in that spiritual space.

Without their help, we were on our own, or rather, I was on my own. With the baby to look after, Donna was usually otherwise engaged. So, I compromised and set to work on a smaller house. I had no plans or blueprints, but I felt like I instinctively knew what to do and how to do it. Almost as if the knowledge was innate: you notch logs, arrange them one on top of each other, secure them with spikes, build your structure, insulate it and live in it! How hard could it be?!

I knew I needed a horse, and I bought her from a nice enough family, although I couldn't help but notice their Mona Lisa smiles while they were selling her to this ignorant city boy from the North End. I soon found out why... She was a giant of a mare—a powerful white animal—but at 9 and a half years, she was old, surly and overweight. I called her Sheba. She didn't do much, except for eat and shit. I wasn't surprised, I had known Italians in my old neighborhood who ate 24/7!

Sheba hadn't let anyone ride her in years, and was so large that I needed a stump or a rock to mount her. She soon figured that out, and would stop 5' from anything I could step on. Quickly I learned to dive over her back, then rotate to face forward.

Without a saddle, I had to learn to ride her bareback. When it worked, we became *one,* with me controlling her with my hand on bridle and mane. She and I would ride into the mountains early mornings, visiting old gold and copper mine shafts where would gaze on tools left by miners of the past.

But most of the time, she stayed rooted to the spot when I told her to move. Or she would set off at a gallop and tried to throw me off. (Just another woman in my life trying to break my balls!) With or without Sheba's help I set to work, envisioning a beautiful log cabin built from the trees I cut down from the National Forest.

I befriended a blacksmith in Merlin, Oregon who gave me a logging fitting for a yoke to put around her. But I learned to ride Sheba without a saddle. It won't surprise you to know that you don't generally learn to ride a horse when you're brought up in the North End, and it's fair to say that we never quite hit it off. Wherever I wanted to go, she pulled me in the other direction. If I wanted to go down into the valley, she led me up the mountain trail.

She would canter innocently up the steep mountainside paths and then, whenever we had to descend, she would set off at a gallop, with me holding onto her mane for dear life, as she reared, jumped, and careered downwards at lightning speeds, then abruptly turn 90º.

We became quite the local tourist attraction: whenever she started rearing up, I looked like the Lone Ranger silhouetted against the sky, albeit a lone ranger in overalls. When they saw me out and about on the horse, people would stop to watch, waiting to see her rear and throw me off again. It was slapstick for the rednecks.

The craziest thing of all was expecting that she'd be cajoled into dragging my felled trees back to the campsite. Encouraging her to pull lumber day after day was pointless. She could drag those logs like toothpicks—if she wanted to—but mostly, she flat out refused. One day, I got so fed up that I slapped her on the arse with a two-by-four.

She snorted at me, and didn't move. In the end I sold Sheba, put on the yoke, and dragged the wood myself. I got enough money from the horse for a 100g bag of brown rice. It might not sound like much rice for a horse, but that bag of rice helped me get through the winter. And when the bugs got into it, as they invariably did, I ate the bugs and got a little extra protein. I'd never have even considered that if we hadn't been so very hungry.

When summer gave way to fall, and the weather started to turn, Donna left with Sarah. She had no intention of staying in the wilderness freezing her ass off, so she took Sarah and to stay with her parents. My instinct was to leave with her, but she convinced me to stay. I felt then as if she might be torturing me by forcing me to endure the cold and the deprivation out there on my own. Nevertheless, I told her with absolute conviction that I'd have made it perfect for them to return to live with me in the Spring.

Even without the horse's help, the house slowly took shape. I built the floor and ceiling—including a sleeping loft—from some second-grade tongue and groove lumber from a local sawmill.

I prepared the land, and planted vegetables, growing fascinated by the cyclical nature of it all: the grasshoppers nibbled at the corn cobs and felled them like little trees. So, then we got chickens to eat the grasshoppers, and then the chickens gave us eggs. The natural order of things was beautifully self-sustaining. Everything felt at one with the environment, except me, of course. I still felt like the ultimate stranger in a strange land. Up until then, I had no idea that vegetables came from the ground. I thought they came from Rosario's Fruit and Vegetables in North End!

With my wolf dog, and horse, I thought only of the necessities of survival. My days were filled with honest toil, and my nights were spent in quiet contemplation. The game of life takes on a wholly different complexion when life is reduced to the bare essentials of sustenance and survival. The work itself was a form of meditation. Every new seed a demonstration of faith.

I worked all through fall and into the winter. The cabin grew slowly while the weather grew wetter. As I discovered, it rains a lot in an Oregon winter. And that is never more apparent than when you're camping out in the wilderness, night after sodden night. And then the cold set in.

When the snow fell, I had to dig through snow and ice to get the mud and the grass to chink the logs. When my gloves wore out, I dug with my bare hands. I lay the logs on top of each other with layers of grass and mud in between for insulation. It made such a tight seal that by the time it was finished, it got so hot when I lit a fire that I had to open the door.

Every night, I tucked myself up in my little garret, quite alone, but quite content in the wilderness. I ate simple meals of brown rice with whatever else I could find. I killed and ate a rattlesnake, and a porcupine. People always ask me what they tasted like, and I can tell you that rattlesnake tasted like... rattlesnake and porcupine tasted like... porcupine! (But at least you don't need a toothpick after eating a porcupine.)

It really was the simplest kind of existence. With my meagre possessions, there were few distractions from the business of living in the moment. I had to read or write by candlelight. And yet, I was quite content. I valued the simple things, like fresh bread. One morning, I made dough, wrapped it in foil and put it in a hole in the ground with hot coals from the fire. When I came home, hours later, the bread was perfectly cooked, and it was the best bread I ever tasted. The next time you're out in the wilderness, I highly recommend 'bread-in-a-hole'.

Not wanting to be too closely associated with the commune, I eventually cut my hair, and shaved my beard off so I didn't look like I belonged with the hippies or the rednecks, but that suited me well enough. Even more importantly, With Donna gone, I was consciously taking away my sexuality, making myself less available, and thus warding off temptation.

The townspeople didn't want anything to do with the hippies, and certainly didn't want them squatting on their land. They put signs in their windows saying: *We do not solicit hippie patronage*! I tried my best to defuse some of the hostility directed towards the commune from the local community.

So, I spoke up on the hippies' behalf, and I listened to the townsfolk's concerns. Gradually we moved towards a more peaceful coexistence between the two sides. The hippies came to think of me as their PR guy, and word spread. I'd always found it easy to draw people to me wherever I went. Partly it was all that artistic training; I knew how to draw in a crowd. But equally, it was something that came easily to us North Enders; the indomitable spirit of North End was alive and well in me and it always craved an audience!

I heard that one of the pastors from the old north church in Boston had been asking after me back at home, and sent word via a minister in Grants Pass, about 40-miles away. He came looking for me at the commune and one of the hippies sent him out into the wilds to find me.

We spent hours together over the next few days, and over the course of our talks on life, religion and philosophy, he decided I had some interesting perspectives. He encouraged more people to come and listen to me talk. It wasn't real-world advice I was dispensing but my own particular brand of cross-faith theoretical theology. I blended Hindu and Christian ideas in ways that people hadn't heard before, and espoused my thoughts on reincarnation and living in God's dream.

The crowds kept getting bigger. People heard about the man in the woods and wanted to learn what they could from me, or challenge me, or cross their ideas with mine. In those days, people were interested in what anybody off-grid or counter cultural had to impart about their life and philosophy. I suppose it's not so different to the YouTube generation; anyone with an angle or an insight can find a crowd of people wanting to listen.

I expected—or rather hoped—that Donna and Sarah would return to live with me in the cabin before we made our next move. When I called Donna to invite her home, she told me she wasn't coming back. It wasn't until I found out that her parents had asked her to leave for having an affair with a black guy—which they disapproved of for reasons in addition to her infidelity—that I knew our time in Oregon was over. I had built the house for our family, but without a family, it meant nothing to me. I gave it away to some local people who had become homeless when the Illinois River had washed their house away, and then I went back to Boston.

The end of the relationship hardly came as a surprise. From stealing Donna from El Cid, through avoiding being drafted, and onto our travels to Jugtown and Oregon, we had barely lived a normal life. But adventure and adrenaline can only take you so far. We had both been so young and naive, and neither of us had stopped to think about what our long-term relationship might have looked like. Beyond the first flush of romance and the illicit excitement of having 'stolen' my girl from a mobster, there was only one thing left that kept us together: our daughter.

The breaking up of that relationship taught me something about attachment and letting go. When you voluntarily put your hand on a hot stove, it takes time for the pain to heal. I spoke to Father Mark, who advised me to be patient after the break-up, to avoid dating, and to just focus on keeping things together. But I was too young and impatient. I was a virile young man in the prime of his life, and I was newly single; it was like being a kid in a candy store, and I couldn't resist the temptation.

In time, Donna's affair fizzled out, and eventually, we decided to try and reconcile for Sarah's sake. It wasn't easy. I had been enjoying the freedom of being an unattached man in the sexually liberated sixties, and committing to monogamy was challenging. In spite of everything, we hoped it would be better for Sarah if we looked past everything that had happened, and committed to co-parenting as a couple.

We moved into a new apartment next to some friends of a man she d dated before. They were all creative types. Alex was an artist and a very heavy drinker, and we enjoyed getting to know our new neighbors. I put in a window right through the building between the two apartments so we could keep an eye on each other's kids more easily instead of getting a babysitter.

It wasn't easy parenting a child when the love has been tried, tested, and found wanting in a relationship, but I labored for my child, and I made sacrifices. I was willing to tolerate all kinds of things to give Sarah a stable home. I was working long hours as a carpenter, and money was tight. We weren't saving much, just paying rent and bills to keep the household running. I partnered with an Irish guy from

South Boston, and we did all kinds of carpentry work: porches, decks, you name it. I wasn't crazy about roof work because of the heights, but I pushed through. We had met in high school, where trade skills were part of the curriculum. He was a straight-A student at Boston Latin but left to explore something different. His search for something *other* helped us become friends. We went on to start a real estate project together, but I backed out at the last minute. Something felt wrong, and shortly afterwards, the economy tanked. My instincts saved me.

More than anything in those days, I was tired. I was basically a zombie by the end of each day because I was working so much overtime. It wasn't much of a life, just keeping the home together, but I found my own fulfilment in it. I continued striving for more, questing and searching beyond myself. Once, when Sarah had a stomach problem, I found that I was able to heal her through sheer willpower. I felt the strength of sacrifice and the grace it brought. When I felt that power, I walked to Sarah's bedroom and placed my hand on her stomach. Then, her pain and crying stopped. Later, I realized this wasn't necessarily about being holy—it felt like more of an untapped mechanical process. It seemed to me that sacrifice can open up a channel for grace, and sometimes healing comes through it. That was a precious moment of absolute spiritual unity between us

I shared no more physical connection with Donna. She stopped wanting to sleep with me, and eventually, I noticed that someone had been using my razor; it was clear then that history was repeating itself. Eventually, I confronted her, and she told me the truth about entering into a relationship with Alex. I told her that I was going to go out for a walk and that by the time I came back she should tell me who she wanted to be with.

I came back and asked the question; she told me that she wanted to be with him. I didn't hate her for it. If anything, I wished her and her new boyfriend luck. I had my own desires to pursue, and plenty of my own mistakes to make. I moved out of that apartment, but before I left, I handed them the keys to the car I'd bought in Oregon. Sarah was going to be living with them, and I wanted to make her life—and by extension theirs—as easy as possible. It was a great car, but they let it sit out on the road and eventually it got towed away thinking it was an abandoned car.

A year or so later, their relationship was over. We'd thought that Alex liked a drink a little too much, but it transpired that he was a full-blown alcoholic, and it had been one of the things that killed their relationship. Donna had started studying to become a nurse, but Alex was directionless; he lived to paint, and he lived for liquor. But there was a dark unquenchable soul in there too, and when his demons grew too powerful, poor Alex made his way out onto the Golden Gate Bridge and jumped off.

CHAPTER 12

Echoes of Other Lifetimes

"I've always been torn between two forces: the passion I feel for God and the passion I feel for women"

I was a little older and wiser when I tried the monastic life again. In my forties, I went to a Greek Orthodox monastery, it was old calendar; very strict. I wanted to see if I could be a Hindu on the inside, employing meditation with the Christian structure of prayer. From my perspective, it worked beautifully, but they didn't see it like that...

Life in the monastery was a very regimented existence. We would have our morning and evening prayers and various jobs to do around the grounds, and in the garden. And we would stand in prayer for three hours or more in the chapel. There was a condition that monks would only be allowed out of the monastery on any little errands if they went in pairs, essentially taking a reminder of monastic life with them. The idea was that it was too dangerous for a monk to be entirely alone in the outside world. I certainly understood that. It wasn't the corruption of the outside world that was the problem, it was the sheer overwhelm. Later in life, there were many times when I was devoting myself to meditation and living an essentially ascetic life when I just wanted to stay in the safety of my little garret, without any distractions. So, if I felt I needed a change of scene, I'd simply drive around the block a time or two, park the car again, and return home because I didn't want to surrender my solitude.

The environment of the Greek Orthodox monastery would have been perfectly conducive to spiritual exploration, but it felt like the same old drill. I already knew that the strict adherence to prayer as the only vehicle to any kind of revelatory experience didn't work for me. So, I would wait until the monks were sleeping, then I would head down to the chapel, focus my breathing, and meditate. Of course, if I heard anyone walking by, I would change my posture to make it look like I was deep in prayer. Meditation just didn't register with the monks who only believed what they read in the Bible. Christ made no mention of meditation, only prayer, ergo, monks don't meditate.

But when I combined those elements of prayer, meditation, and mindful breathing, I took off like a rocket. The energy and the power of standing in prayer for hours was like my rocket fuel, thousands of pounds of reason and logic representing the booster rockets which had to be dropped in order for the silent engines of meditation to engage and pierce the stratosphere. It felt to me as if our souls want to complete their journey to their source, like salmon returning to the waterways where they were spawned, and that's where my meditations were leading me.

It was a blissful experience. In the height of meditative ecstasy, all I could say was "Take me." I started seeking every opportunity to let my mind fly, untethered by its self-imposed restraints. Later, a Dutch woman philosopher (and a lover of mine) would sometimes take me into her dreams. I'd call her the next day and say, 'We were in Europe together,' and she'd confirm she'd decided to take me along with her on her astral journey. These experiences taught me something about consciousness, and how it isn't bound by the usual rules we think govern reality.

Years later, when I told one of my friends about my meditative experiences, she asked, "What were you smoking?" To her, the idea of attaining that kind of bliss without any other stimulation seemed utterly outrageous. But the dangers of meditative addiction were just as serious. And, like any addict, if I got high on meditation, I'd always want to go even higher, like any other addict chasing the next hit.

Even the sacrifices I made—like fasting, or giving up something I enjoyed—began to feel like ways of making each hit better. If I saw someone suffering, I wouldn't eat for a day, thinking that my small sacrifice might help them on some cosmic, karmic scale. But even in those acts of selflessness, I'd catch myself feeling pride, taking pleasure in my own generosity. And that's the trap, isn't it? What do we do when the selflessness becomes its own reward? When ascetism reveals itself as false and brings its own pleasures, when every 'sacrifice' takes you closer to the euphoria of the Divinity, then you know you're trapped between sobriety and excess.

Shakespeare said, "They are as sick that surfeit with too much as they that starve with nothing." I knew exactly what he meant.

I tried to stay centered. But what do you do when life outside of meditation feels hollow? As always, my thoughts turned to women. Of course, I understood the basic principles of monastic life—why men and women are separated in that environment—but I came to realize that, on a deeper level, it was because monks and nuns had to be married to God.

I was reminded of the poet and mystic, William Blake, who suggested that when he made love to my wife, he could sense God sticking his head in through the window. That seemed to me a beautiful way of saying it. I felt—and still feel—that it's possible to balance the two, but sometimes things get mixed up. And if we carry karmic residue from past lives it makes things even more complicated. Perhaps we're paying back an emotional or spiritual debt for past indulgences, physical, emotional, or otherwise. And maybe part of why we're here is to learn how to love God perfectly.

That constant tension between spiritual and worldly love became my own particular cross to bear. So I carried on living like a monk, fasting for days, avoiding women entirely, staying celibate. And every time pride reared its head, and I wavered in my convictions, I felt like an alcoholic falling off the wagon. Then I succumbed all over again to the pursuit of the physical. The depth of my addiction to worldly pleasure was compelling, and like any other addict, one woman was never enough. Moderation never worked for me. Breaking my abstinence felt like unleashing the animal. I must have dated a United Nations worth of women. And then I would recant and retreat back into abstinence.

Like Merton himself, I discovered that the heart follows its own path. When he was recuperating from debilitating back pain in a Louisville hospital, Merton fell in love with a 19-year old student nurse, Margie Smith. Merton documented the relationship—which lasted several months—in Volume 6 of his journals: *Learning to Love*, and it led him to seriously question his monastic vocation. He came to view this love as another manifestation of Divine grace, refusing to interpret them as oppositional forces, but as complementary ones that enhanced his understanding of the intersection between human and Divine experiences.

For much of my life, I had wondered if it was even possible to love God and a woman equally. Growing up, the choices seemed stark. Either you got married, raised a family, and focused on earthly attachments, or you took vows of celibacy and walked the monastic path. I never saw why the two paths had to be so separate. Why couldn't they coexist? Why couldn't love for a woman also deepen my connection to the Divine?

But whenever I had tried to reconcile them, it all unraveled. I kept falling in love, over and over again, and it became an addiction. I chased one, and then another, and another... Each new relationship felt like it would complete me, like it would be the one to settle the storm, but it never did. Instead, I found myself tangled in chaos—not knowing how to mix that passion for the Divine with the passion for worldly intimacy.

I never understood why I was struggling so much. I didn't realize that my approach to love, like my approach to God, was too attached to the idea of what I thought it should be. I didn't understand the nature of detachment, of loving without clinging. Even now, I'm still learning that true love isn't about possession or dependence—it's about letting go.

Thomas Merton's story resonated deeply with me. Here was a man who spent 26 years in a monastery, dedicating his life to God, and then fell in love. It must have felt to him like an entirely new discovery, but maybe it wasn't. Maybe it was something he'd always known, deep down, but hadn't allowed himself to feel until then. That's how it was for me

Every time I fell in love, it felt brand new, like I was discovering love for the first time. But the truth is, I'd been there before. For so long, I felt I was walking in circles in the woods, repeating the same patterns without advancing at all. I'd pour my passion into God, into women, into striving to understand the universe, only to feel like I ended up right back where I started.

Finally, I realized it wasn't a circle, it was a spiral. Each time I returned to the same point, I was moving upward, gaining new insights, even if the progress felt painfully slow. The helix of life has a way of bringing us back to the same spot, over and over, but at a different elevation each time. So, even if the view may feel the same, the perspective is always just a little different.

This slow ascent, this helix, is another reason why I believe we have so many lifetimes. Each one adds another layer of understanding. Through meditation, I've felt glimpses of those lifetimes, as if the experiences of countless incarnations were filtering back to me. It's why I value meditation so deeply—not just as a way to calm the mind but as a means of drawing upon the wisdom of lived experience from the past.

Even now, I think perhaps the tension between these two loves—Divine and human—was necessary for my growth, just as it had been for Merton's understanding of the struggle between the worldly and the spiritual. Maybe you need both the sacred and the profane, the spirit and the flesh, to make a complete human being.

Monastic life didn't work for me. The pure Catholic ideology and mine didn't mesh. But those people had such a passion and a love for God that it filled the space. You could almost touch it. And I realized that at its simplest, religion is just a vehicle, it's a car. And when your family or your friends come to visit you, you don't care what cars they're driving. You just want them to reach you, however they can.

I left the monastery believing in the power of my discoveries, and resolved to live my life worrying less about my 'car' and more about the purity of my love for God. But that didn't make the journey any easier. The struggle between Divine love and human passion continued, each new relationship feeling like another turn in the spiral, another opportunity to learn the same lessons in a slightly different way. I realized I was seeking something impossible: a perfect resolution between spiritual and worldly love. Nevertheless, I remained fixated by the conflict, veering from one extreme to another.

The same was true for my creative work. In later years as an artist, my work was always a mix of reason and intuition, geometric forms meeting the chaos of freeform. I'd dream of designs before building them, guided by something I couldn't fully explain. That metaphor of the booster rockets of a shuttle applies here too: reason and logic provided the lift, but eventually, they had to be jettisoned for the craft to soar higher. It was only by letting go of those rational anchors that I could reach new levels of creativity.

The lesson, I think, is the same for love and spirituality. You have to let go of attachment—not just to people or things, but even to the idea of God. As the Buddhist's appreciate, as long as you're clinging to a concept, you're stuck. When we get attached to something we think will make us happy—an idea, an object, or a relationship—it often turns out to be an illusion. As soon as we try to grab hold of it, it slips away, like smoke through our fingers. It's all part of the illusion we live in.

In Hinduism, they say that life itself is like a Divine screen, and when we die, we wake up, realizing this existence was like a dream. It's like seeing our life in a movie theater: we get totally engrossed in the story, our emotions pulled in all directions, but when the credits roll, we step outside into the real world, and suddenly the film feels distant, unreal.

It takes countless lifetimes to evolve and truly grasp this concept. Thomas Merton once said that the best way to become a contemplative or mystic isn't necessarily through retreating from the world into monasteries or caves. It's about engaging with the world and learning from the messiness of life itself. True freedom comes from detachment, even from your own notions of what God is supposed to be.

I've come to realize that I don't need to rush this process. Like McCloskey told me about my voice, I need to keep it relaxed, let it evolve naturally. Every time I try to force my growth, I lose something essential. If I get too high in meditation, I want to go even higher, chasing the next hit, instead of relishing the experience in the moment. So, I had to learn that forcing it only creates tension. Relaxation is key—not just for the voice, but for the soul.

And maybe that's why God leaves some of us to figure things out on our own. I always admired the work of Henry Rousseau. Despite his "primitive" style that was ridiculed by the cognoscenti of the art world, his work went on to influence Picasso and the surrealist movement. He did away with the conventions of perspective and proportion, but still managed to achieve the sort of authenticity that many other artists' more detailed work completely failed to do.

I discovered that same tension between formal teachings and lived experience in the writings of the Desert Fathers of early Christianity, who prized direct spiritual experience over formal theological education. I read about the Zen concept of "beginner's mind" (shoshin) which went so far as to suggest how formal training can actually become a barrier to genuine insight. I felt Rousseau's journey exemplified Zen practitioners' "don't-know mind." And to me it suggested that spiritual truth, like artistic truth, might sometimes be more accessible to those who find their own way rather than following established paths.

In that spirit, I was happy to go on figuring out life without a guide. Rather than a hindrance to progress, I chose to see it as a measure of my beginner's mind at work. I didn't want to have all the answers handed to me. I chose instead to embrace every misstep and every imperfection; to learn slowly.

I've realized, too, that we're not all living perfect lives, precisely because God loves a good drama. Life is all about the story, the messiness, the humanity. That's why Christ didn't choose perfect disciples. He picked fishermen, tax collectors, and misfits—people full of flaws, illiterates, nobodies. The world isn't perfect, so how could the church or its people be? The imperfections are what make it all so compelling. What a dramatist!

As I moved forward into marriage, business ventures, fatherhood, and all my other adventures, these early struggles with balancing the spiritual and the worldly never really left me, but I knew then that they weren't supposed to. The tension itself was the point - the creative force that kept pushing me to grow, to seek, to understand.

I think there is comfort in knowing that spiritual discovery isn't about perfect adherence to doctrine or ritual, but is only about the authenticity of the connection. That's what I was seeking in my long hours of meditation, in the combination of prayer and breathing practices, in my own particular way of reaching for the Divine. And when the spiritual practices I was leaning on become attachments too, I had to be willing to let go of them, and let go of any ideas I had about what spirituality should look like. As Christ said: "Let your right hand not know what your left hand is doing." There's a very subtle way of being absolutely free, but to achieve it, you have to let go.

Even now, as I keep learning, keep discovering, and keep growing, I have come to realize that I don't need to rush this process. Like McCloskey told me about my voice, I need to keep it relaxed, let it evolve naturally. Every time I try to force my growth, I lose something essential. Forcing it only creates tension. Relaxation is key—not just for the voice, but for the soul.

Chapter 13

Balancing Logic and Intuition

"Sometimes the path to enlightenment leads through darkness"

I was single. I was free to pursue whatever kind of life felt right to me in the moment. So, when my friends Perry and Keiko invited me to rent the top floor of their house in Cambridge, I accepted gladly. They both moved in the local artists' circles and had been impressed by my work. Inspired by the freedom to create art for art's sake, I started to work in the field of sculpture and ceramics. As well as being a sculptor, Perry was a metallurgist at M.I.T., working with historical techniques for joining metals. Keiko was a visual artist who did large-scale installations, like the sculptural lights she created for the city of Boston.

I pored myself into my work and allowed it to consume me. Beyond work, I gave myself over to celibacy. For a year, I sought no physical intimacy. I plunged deep into a monastic phase, barely even thinking about excess of any kind. Purged of physical desires, eating pure and simple foods, and focussing on my spiritual journey through reading and meditation, I felt closer to Divinity than ever before.

Feeling that close to God was euphoric. Through prayer and meditation, I felt joy and peace, free from attachments. I wanted to free myself from the desire for sex that I had struggled with in the past. I'd seen so many people in miserable relationships, hating each other after the first year, and wanted to be liberated from it. The struggle persisted, as I continued to devote myself to finding equilibrium, still experimenting with the idea that it must be possible to be with a woman and love God at the same time. But, instead of balance I found that periods of excess and abstinence followed each other like the changing seasons. It was always one extreme or the other.

That's when I met Andrea, and it stirred something deep inside me. After many months of near solitude and absolute celibacy, my need for intimacy reasserted itself, strongly. That first night with Andrea, we had dinner, went to bed together, and had sex. I felt immense guilt afterward, as though I had broken a vow to God, like a monk breaking his vow of celibacy. That very night, I had a dream in which I was a woman with long black hair, kneeling at the feet of Christ. His presence was so powerful that I started to cry on his feet. I wiped my tears off his feet with my long, black hair. The next morning, I woke up feeling like I had been forgiven for my sins through multiple lifetimes. It was as though I'd been given a green light to move forward with the relationship.

Andrea was a writer, and had been a pen pal of Anaïs Nin, the French writer known for her diaries in the '30s and '40s. When I met her, Andrea was getting her master's at Boston University. In the early 1970s, she got into a doctoral program in Colorado, so we moved there for her to finish her degree. We rented a little house in Denver, and I took on side jobs. I made furniture for people, and helped them move; I did whatever was needed. We had an old milk truck that we bought in Maine from Oakhurst Dairy. It was the kind you drive standing up, with folding doors. The front looked like a giant Volkswagen, but it could carry 20 tons of milk. That's what I drove, hauling everything all the way from Maine to Boulder, Colorado.

The relationship with Andrea turned out to be tough. She eventually had an affair with one of her students. Having been given the green light to proceed with the relationship in a dream, the presentiment of its demise came to me in a dream as well. In the dream, she was dancing around a crazy man who was trying to kill her with a knife. I tried to pull her away, but she wouldn't listen. I awoke the next morning to a knock at the door, and when I looked through the curtains, I saw that it was the man from my dream. A voice in my head said, "You have to open the door. What has to happen will happen." So, I opened the door, and he told me he was one of her students. As they walked away, I sat in a meditative position and thought, *Let this end quickly. Let me find the strength to move on to the next phase of my life.* After four or five years of being together, we separated.

It took me a year to process everything and become philosophical about it. Initially, I was angry—angry at Andrea and angry at God. I had thought I'd been given God's approval to commit to that relationship, and I felt betrayed by them both. But eventually, I realized it was part of karma, a punishment or lesson from a past life. It's hard to be philosophical about your past misdeed when they hurt you in the present, but in time, I was able to reflect on it with more clarity.

After Colorado, I felt Boston calling me home. I settled in Cambridge with its intellectuals, its energy, and its potential. It was such a fluid, dynamic place. And I felt like I was home. It was a cauldron of thought, ambition, and philosophy.[23] I've always felt that I've lived in New England before. Whenever I see Samuel Adams in those portraits, I feel a strange hatred for him as if our paths crossed in a previous life. His contemporaries certainly described him as cold, aloof, and condescending, and whenever I look at one of his portraits, I instinctively think, *What an asshole!*[24]. I won't even drink the beer because of it. I simply, deeply feel that I can't stand him.

*

One day, Keiko and I went to a gallery opening in Cambridge, and that's where I first saw Mary. She later told me she was staring at me the whole time we were there. At the time, she was married then to a professor at M.I.T.—a literature scholar and head of his department—so nothing happened immediately. But after her marriage ended, we became very close, very quickly.

---

[23] The Cambridge intellectual scene of the 1970s was marked by interdisciplinary exchange between Harvard, MIT, and independent scholars. Regular salons and discussion groups bridged the gap between academic and counter-cultural thinking.

[24] Samuel Adams may have been regarded as a patriot, but he was also a legendarily intolerant Puritan, opposed to any sort of fun! He had it in for theater, dancing, and many popular entertainments. The beer company named after him was only founded in 1984.

Our connection was instant, and electric. Mary was ten years older than me, and, not long after we met, she told me, "I got very excited when I was 10-years old because I knew you were born." We had very different backgrounds, but she said our brains fit together perfectly. Of course, mine was an untrained brain, whereas her brain was the acme of academic achievement. She found Harvard easy. She got the third highest score in the country when she was just toying with the idea of going into medicine.

We would start out our mornings together with Aristotle, Spinoza, Zeno, and a coterie of philosophers and thinkers. Sometimes, she would look at me, wonder in her eyes and say, "You just explained in two sentences what Zeno's followers had been arguing about for 500 years." We had the perfect synthesis of schooled intellect and intuitive thinking. Her academic rigor helped me articulate what I knew instinctively, while my street-level spirituality brought philosophical concepts down to earth. Our time together was marked by this constant interplay of the intellectual and the intuitive. I was bringing my world into hers, and she was helping me understand my experiences through a more academic lens.

Through Mary, I was suddenly surrounded by academics and department heads. They were crazy and wonderful people—just an eclectic mix. The dinner parties we hosted were something else; like philosophical salons mixed with North End energy—profound discussions punctuated by bursts of laughter and music. There were anthropologists, Irish musicians with penny whistles, and plenty of wine from Jobies on Beacon Hill. The conversation was wild, the food was gourmet, and everyone got gloriously drunk. It was a grand time, and those characters—though most of them are gone now—still linger in my memory.

Some were absolutely insane, like the heiress to the Loomis family fortune, worth hundreds of millions. If you invited her over for dinner, she'd bring half a bottle of wine, despite owning houses in New York, Europe, and Boston. As the Italians say, "Some people have very short arms—they can't reach their pockets."

There were the Van Vactors: David was this brilliant man who got into every Ivy League school: Harvard, Yale, Princeton. He came from a family of composers and Southern oil wealth. But his life was unconventional, to say the least. He had an affair with his sister, Raven, that lasted decades, starting in their youth. She, in turn, had a strange relationship with their father. It was outrageously unconventional.

David was also a champion wrestler at Harvard, though I did manage to pin him once. We were at a dinner party—about a dozen people at our house—and for some reason, we decided to wrestle. Everyone pushed their chairs aside to watch. He almost had me, but I pulled a quick reversal and got him pinned. His wife, Pat, joked afterward, "Now I know who to call when David gets out of hand."

Pat and David were French gourmet cooks who once convinced a Greek diner to let them open a French restaurant at night. It was wildly successful—for two days. We cooked, ate, drank, and had the time of our lives, but eventually, the Greeks shut it down.

I even met John Kenneth Galbraith through these circles. Nancy Sweezy, who was divorced from Paul Sweezy—the prominent Marxist economist at Harvard—introduced me to him. I would sometimes have breakfast with Nancy and her friends when they were visiting. The whole Cambridge scene opened up a new world of ideas and connections.

My friend Paul, who went on to be an MIT liaison to the government, became blind at the age of five. He was brilliant, was awarded multiple doctorates, and had a great sense of humor. His phone number ended in 2020! And he loved joking about his "perfect vision." He worked with Andrea Bocelli on developing a GPS system for the blind. Even in our neighborhood of characters, Paul stood out—not for his disability, but for how he transformed it into opportunity. (It always occurred to me that when a man is blind, he believes others to be blind as well, by the nature of narcissism. Unknown to him, his face reads like a map for all those who can see.)

Even in this rarefied intellectual atmosphere, I never lost touch with my core self. The street smarts I'd developed in North End served me well in academic circles. I could hold my own in discussions about Heidegger while still maintaining the practical wisdom I'd learned from the wiseguys. It was an interesting balance—being able to discuss existential philosophy over morning coffee, then spend the afternoon in my workshop creating sculpture, followed by an evening of entertaining academics with stories from the North End.

With my artistic endeavors expanding—and my commissions extending to large-form pieces, I moved out of the basement and bought and restored my father's property. I installed a workshop there, and had a large studio—the entire top floor with a southern exposure—above the Bank of America in North End where I would just think and draw. They had a Sacco Vanzetti plaque attached to the front of the building, because they used to have their Anarchist meetings there. But one thing they always argued about: "If we're truly anarchists, surely we shouldn't be having meetings?!"

I gave shape and form to my ideas in my own workshop, full of industrial machinery I had welding equipment—oxyacetylene, TIG, and MIG—and a controlled atmosphere with argon gas. I even had the city of Boston dig up the streets to bring three-phase power to my workshop to run the Bridgeport milling machine and other heavy equipment.

Fueled by creativity—and now also fueled by a harmonious relationship with Mary, as opposed to an ever-questing relationship with God—I expanded my artistic enterprise. I could work in any material: metal, wood, glass—whatever the piece called for. They were mostly free-form, largely abstract. Some were furniture-like, others purely artistic. I used the foundries at MassArt to cast pieces, many in aluminum. I got into casting and began participating in art shows and taking commissions.

I did sculptural functional pieces for restaurants, and more figurative work, and most of all, I loved working in abstract forms because making something look like something—a tree or a person—felt meaningless to me. Abstract work allowed me to deal in symbolism. That's why I liked to mix freeform expression with the structural logic of cubism. I combined geometric precision with free-form madness.

It's like in tool and die making, where we'd work to a tolerance of one-tenth of a thousandth of an inch. If you took a thousandth of an inch off, you'd have to throw the piece away. It was like splitting a human hair lengthways, ten times over; the slightest mistake would ruin everything. We'd measure everything with light projections onto a screen rather than physical tools, like calipers, to gauge radii and other forms.

I realized that if you get the foundation absolutely perfect, you can go as crazy as you want with freeform expression because you always have that solid reference point. For me, it was about balancing physical laws with wild, intuitive forms. A lot of my work reflected this continuous theme of logic versus madness, structure versus freeform. I realized, while working on these pieces, that I was really working on myself, externalizing my inner struggles. So I applied this principle to my art and my life; a strong and steady base allowed for free expression.

Each piece was unique, with no strict protocol. My portfolio was strictly eclectic; every piece turned out differently. If you lined my pieces up, side by side, you would never know that the same artist had shaped them all. Sometimes ideas came from dreams, sometimes from sketches made before or after the piece was created. (I know that sketches typically predate the actual work, but I sometimes did it the other way around.) The one consistent thing was my inconsistency. I'd get bored very easily and move on to something else, constantly starting new artistic adventures.

A stockbroker commissioned me to create a special hearth for his fireplace. His brief was very simple, but I couldn't help but take it further. I made it out of mahogany and slate with brass corners which dovetailed into the wood. It turned out beautifully. After rushing to finish it for his party, he asked to delay payment because he'd just bought a sailboat. With quiet conviction, I told him, "No, you're paying me now." The ghost of an earlier version of me reared up unbidden and then surfaced again. Sure enough, he paid the money, and that was the end of that.

One candelabra I made for a client on the West Coast was over six feet tall, made of brass and metal. She said it helped her healing process, which affirmed for me that art has a power to affect people in profound ways. I was fascinated by pre-Christian symbols, like the crucifix, which represents the unity of heaven (the vertical line) and earth (the horizontal line). These ancient symbols often inspired my work. The materials and elements I used—copper, brass, steel, silver, glass, fire—all played into the personality of each piece too. When each piece was complete, it felt alive, as if it had an energy field.

My art sustained me, spiritually, creatively, and financially. I often worked through dreams. I would dream about pieces, redesigning them in my sleep, like one commission where I reimagined and rebuilt the work differently than the original drawing I'd shown. The result was better, but sometimes people wanted exactly what was on paper. For instance, I had a commission for a backdrop for the Holy Monstrance at St. Anthony's, a Catholic church in Boston. I made it out of African mahogany and Italian gold leaf, but I took creative liberties, and they didn't accept it until I remade it to the original specifications. Ironically, the first version was the one that worked best on the altar.

My dreams were even more potent when my own fasting felt like a homage to Catholic fasts. And it seemed to me that every Easter, I'd experience an artistic breakthrough. It was as if there was something about that time that inspired my creative rebirth, whether it was mirroring Christ's rebirth, or the sense of change and renewal in the natural world, or just memories of times growing up in North End where Easier celebrations—kids in white, church bells ringing, Italians smoking cigars and drinking espresso[25]—felt magical. I would slip into a trance-like state, and new thoughts and artistic ideas started coming to me in an ecstasy of discovery.

I often felt that something beyond me directed my work. I was the antenna to receive the energy or consciousness that wanted to come through. I once made a table from huge oak railroad ties. The top piece was almost 12-inches thick. I carved it and included three pre-Christian symbols on the top and medieval crucifixes on the sides. I didn't consciously set out to make it resemble an altar, but that's how most people perceived it.

As well as taking private commissions, I often exhibited my work. I

---

[25] Sadly, many of those traditions have faded with the influx of yuppies who complained about the bells, and had no sense of connection to the old Italian traditions we kept alive.

preferred creating a body of work for a show rather than taking very specific commissions because of the freedom it gave me to follow my instincts. With commissions, there was always someone looking over my shoulder.

At one show, a doctor bought every single piece except one. It felt a little forlorn without its fellow works, but then he came back later to buy that piece too. Some of my work was shown in high-end galleries, and I enjoyed playing with people's perceptions in selecting the pieces for display. I knew that, had they been shown anywhere else, some of the pieces I chose might have been tossed in the rubbish. But I liked the conceit that being shown in a high-end gallery conferred extra status to any piece. The cachet of the venue enhanced the artwork and gave it additional value. But that's art for you!

I opened an art gallery near Louisburg Square and put on art shows, wanting to combine the visual with the performing arts as one movement in time and space. I would make a stage out of my vacuum press, putting together 3-piece ensembles from one of my favorite periods: Italian Baroque.

My youngest daughter Ariel lived with me during the summer months. I enrolled her in Walnut Hill School for the Arts during the summer, where she studied ballet, and where I discovered some of her young prodigy musician friends. All three were young beautiful women like Ariel, which contributed to the magical equation of what was about to happen...

During the shows the crowds were so immense, cars couldn't get over Beacon Hill. Mary (who was department head at the Sculpture/Art Institute of Boston at the time) was blown away by the electricity of the events. She would say, "What the fuck's going on here?!" Of course, cases of wine helped!

The creative process became a form of meditation for me. When I was fully immersed in my work, time would disappear. It was like those hours I spent as a child watching the sun move across my room, but now I was actively participating in creation rather than just observation. Each piece became a dialogue between my technical skill and something larger than myself, call it inspiration, the Divine, or simply the creative force that moves through everything.

The same streak of creativity that ran through my artistic work surfaced throughout my life. Like the disappearing shower I built in one of my apartments. The units were tiny, only about 600 square feet, so conserving space was critical. I built a movie theater that disappeared into the ceiling, and the shower was hidden in the floor—completely invisible until you needed it. I installed a hydraulic lift that took you up onto the roof, featuring hidden skylights from Denmark that turned the space into a secluded balcony. None of it was out of a magazine; I just thought it up.

This creative drive always connected to something deeper. When I wrote about my work, I did it only after the piece was complete. During creation, I stayed connected to the intuitive process, as if I were "pregnant" with the idea. The writing came later, when I could analyze how the materials, forms, and my emotions all connected and when I could see more clearly how the art had also revealed something about myself.

It was like what I learned about true voice from McCloskey. Just as he taught me that the real voice could only emerge when the body was completely relaxed, I discovered that true creativity could only flow when I stopped forcing it. The same principle applied to meditation and prayer—you had to let go of trying to control the outcome.

Every piece I created became a kind of prayer, a meditation on form and spirit. Like the altar piece I made with the railroad ties and Christian symbols. One day, one of my tenants wanted me to meet her friend, Margie. The first thing Margie did was put her feet up on the altar. Immediately, my head started to spin, and I felt like someone was trying to push me out of my body or out of who I was. I was grasping for a sense of myself. Suddenly, Margie let out a sigh and said, "Wow, you're the strongest person I've ever come up against." Then she added, "I have to tell you—I'm a witch.' She asked me, "Are you a witch?" I heard myself respond, "Yes."

That experience taught me something about the power objects can hold. It wasn't just about creating beautiful forms—the pieces themselves could become vessels for energy, for transformation. Each material had its own spirit, its own way of working with the Divine creative force. I realized I was following the same pattern I'd discovered in the Trinity: it was a melding of thought, motion, and creation. Each piece began as an idea, moved through the physical process of creation, and emerged as something new. The process of conceiving and making art was just as much about participating in the creative force that moves through everything.

That's why I preferred working alone. In solitude, I could align myself with that force and become a channel for it without ever feeling as if I was under scrutiny or working to somebody else's time constraints. It was like those moments in the monastery when I combined prayer with meditation; my best work came from combining technical precision with spiritual openness.

One piece which exemplified all my thinking was a giant wooden multi-axial sphere, about four feet wide, that hung from my ceiling. It served as a sort of diary. Inside were nested spheres that I could align based on how I felt—yesterday, today, or tomorrow. When they all aligned, I felt like the energy flowed perfectly.

Looking back now, I see how every sculpture, every innovative solution, every creative act was part of the same journey. Whether I was welding metal or carving wood, installing hidden showers or building meditation benches, I was always trying to make the invisible visible, to give form to spirit.

Between my adventures in business and art, I found myself constantly moving between different worlds. One day I'd be theorizing over morning coffee with Mary, the next I'd be in the workshop with my industrial machinery, working on something sculptural, twisting materials to fit my vision. Mary appreciated how my artwork bridged the spiritual and material worlds. She saw how I combined geometric precision with free-form madness. She encouraged me to find those moments of deeper understanding, when I felt as if my ideas really connected to larger themes about beauty and transcendence.

The Cambridge years with Mary taught me something essential about balance. In North End, everything was immediate, visceral, lived in the moment. In the academic world, everything was analyzed, considered, viewed through various theoretical lenses. I learned to move between these two worlds, to see how they informed each other. The street wisdom of the North End often contained profound truths that philosophers had spent centuries trying to articulate, while academic insights helped me understand my own intuitive knowledge in new ways.

I found a third way, a middle way. A less travelled path that wound between those man-made boundaries and led me somewhere else. Somewhere closer to the Divine.

<u>Celebrating the Italian Feast in North End.</u>

Peter, the tough North End street kid at 7-years-old.

An Italian wedding (about 1949). To this day, I still remember how beautiful that little Italian girl was! And I remember my mother's iron grip on my arm, trying to keep me away from her!

Saint Stephen's Church. Peter at 15 years old digging for clams in Cape Cod.

Arigo Selvitella was the Boss of Bosses, old school man of honor. He was known as the peace maker, holding court at the old Florentine on Hanover St. People would wait to have counsel/sit downs with Arigo. He was a family of my family, I would often see him at the bar in my family's restaurant. When I was 15 years old, he was in his 70's. One day I heard the guys arguing over a sports game at my family's restaurant bar. I then heard Arigo say, "Who cares? They don't put any money in my pocket."

[ARIGO SELVITELLA]

AND

After Arigo went into retirement the Angiulo's, Gennaro and his brothers took over. At the time a lot of young Italians were becoming hooked on drugs. So the Angiulo's put several mobsters in charge of cleaning the streets of users and dealers. One night, my wife and I returned home to find our neighbor on the first floor warning me there had been two men, covered in blood, who said they were looking for me. Our neighbor said, "The soft spoken one told me to tell you they were ging to kill you!" Because I had longish hair and a short beard they'd assumed I was a drug -using hippie. When my family heard about it, they spoke with the Boss of Bosses, Arigo Selvitella who stopped it immediately!

After that, I remember walking by those mobsters who had been friends before getting their orders to eliminate me. I could see in their eyes the frustration that they had to exert self-control, and also the bewilderment as to why they were stopped.

 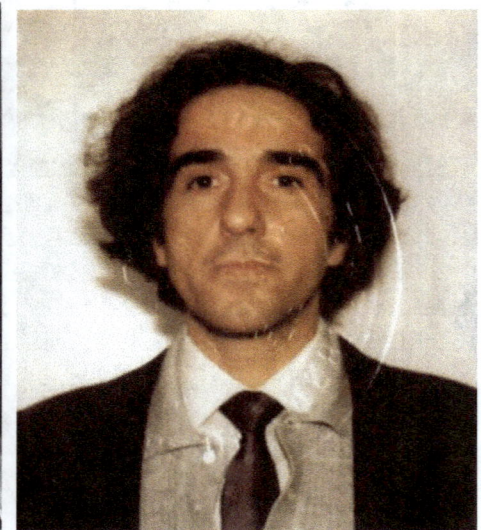

A young Peter's ID photo.

My friend (Fred) in the photo, needed three women to work in his downtown Boston office for a couple of days, (he only had two). So, I offered to dress up as an Indian woman, making the third. On the last day (without thinking) I walked into the men's room, unwrapped my sarees (with my regular clothes underneath) wrapped the sarees under my arm left the building. Fred told me, everyone was asking, "Whatever happened to the Indian woman who walked into the men's room and never walked out again?"

Another funny thing: as we (and two other women) were walking down Hanover Street on one of our workdays, while I was still dressec in the saree, there was a group of Italian guys hanging out at the street corner. One of the guys (Joe DeLuca) turned to look me straight in eye and said, "Hi Peter, and then without missing a beat, turned back around and continued talking to the guys like nothing ever happened.

Embarking on our new life in Oregon. At first, we lived in a tent.

Cutting the wood to build our cabin. The horse that tried to break my balls, Sheba!

The cabin in construction and finally, completed.

Riding Sheba, with my daughter, Sarah.

The cabin the depths of the Oregon Winter.

Beautiful... but very cold!

Yeti, my wolf dog.

Hunting.

After my haircut.

I put windows in the log cabin loft where I slept.

Four views of my wooden Multiple Axis Spheres, about 4' feet in diameter. I used it as a daily diary, because I could see how I felt the day/s before by how I positioned the spheres on that particular day. I was fascinated by how it could be folded absolutely flat and then be pulled out in multiple directions, it reminded me of the cartoons I watched as a child, how the character in the cartoon could draw a door on the wall and then open it. Maybe it was the divine ability of creating something out of nothing.

These 4 sculptures have a symbiotic relationship because one came from the other. Each subsequent piece was made from the left-over pieces and scraps of the preceding piece.

Oak Altar. I always had a special reverence for oak, it was my choice for furniture making for years, I would sometimes chew the Oak wood shavings.

I made the Altar out of old oak railroad ties, that withstood harsh conditions, rain, heat, snow, and the mechanical impact of heavy train loads.

It suffered. I used only hand tools in the making, carved pre-Christian symbols on the top and carved Celtic crosses on the legs.

In many cultures, oaks were associated with gods of lightning and divine rulers, were often struck by lightning, and were seen as a symbol of closeness to the Divine.

This is the table that Margie (the Witch) put her feet up on, which you'll read about in this book.

The African mahogany and Italian gold leaf pieces were a commission from the Catholic archdiocese in downtown Boston it was a backdrop for the Holy Monstrous where they kept the Holy Eucharist, the Body and Blood of Christ. It took me 5-minutes to draw the design for the commission presentation in one of my two studios in North End. I had the whole floor above the Bank of America where I would think and draw, while Mafia violence was happening on Hanover St below. True Italian Yoga at its best!

The first image shows the original design.

The second and third images show the final design. When working on the piece, I deviated from the original design and followed the design of my heart. The church said "NO! We want the original design!" After I finished making the original design, we placed both on the church altar and the one that worked the best was the one I made with poetic liberty.

I made this 6' Weeping Brass Blcod of Christ candelabra out of iron, copper, brass, bronze and silver with the. I made it from the beds of Nuns (St Joseph order) the convent next to my studio.

Mary, my Harvard-ex and I had another couple over for dinner, the husband who was a colleague of Mary's had his own architectural firm in Cambridge. He said, "Peter, there's an architectural magazine with architect-designed candelabras and your pieces are more beautiful than any candelabra I have ever seen!"

These are three images of the same piece. It's a study in perspective; how one piece could change dramatically into many by the influence of perspective. (This could only be achieved by painting the base white!) Made from steel and brass.

Cyclops - glass, brass, copper, silver.

I had designed a fastening system (for the followers of the famous architect, Buckminster Fuller) to be used on geodesic dome. It worked using a 12-faced shape (dodecahedron. After working the equations on a computer, a Yale mathematician said it's not possible because the dihedral angle of a regular dodecahedron is approximately 116.565"

However, I proved him wrong by physically making the "impossible" piece using a block of wood. When I showed him the working dodecahedron adapter with the precise angles needed, he was overwhelmec with joy because this breakthrough meant larger structures could now be built using smaller dodecahedron building blocks. It lent credence to Zeno's theorem that the door is never closed. What does this have to do with Cyclops?

The Buckminister Fuller people were blinded snobs thinking all things have to follow formal protocol in their origin. The next morning, I went in for an early meeting, having created Cyclops the evening before with no mathematical equation. They arrived earlier than me, and when I opened the door, I saw that they'd placed a large card on top of Cyclops that said ... BRAVO!

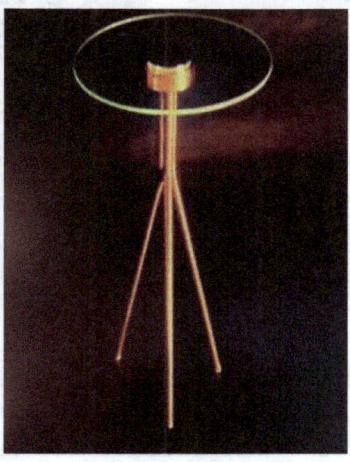

I was able to weld different exotic metals together with controlled atmosphere. I couldn't make these fast enough, selling them in the high-end art galleries.

Cast aluminium.

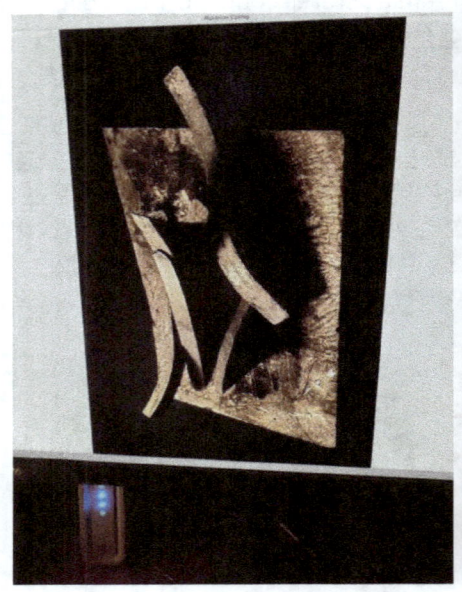
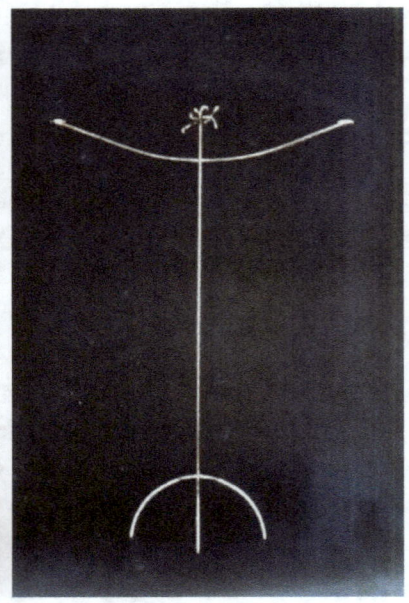

Medusa. A 6' sculptural candelabra made out of iron, brass, bronze, and silver. The Iron is also from the beds of the covenant nuns, the Sisters of St Joseph. I only polished the tips of the brass/bronze Medusa head, so when the candles flames flickered, the Medusa head seem to move in the light and shadows.

Flying Octopus, looks like glass. It can change its colors, depending on the environmental lighting (maybe due to the chemical adhesive) that brought out it's rainbow colors, becoming part of its aesthetical function like an Octopus changing its color, depending on its environment.

<u>Altar - Cherry.</u>

<u>I designed the altar in 3 pieces (top and 2 Legs) with a machine screw locking system that would snap together with a one turn of the machine screws, locking it tight as one solid piece. In some testimonials, people not only loved the aesthetics, but also the locking system design, making all 3 sections one solid piece (a Trinity).</u>

<u>Wooden table design.</u>

Very heavy, solid, aluminium wall piece I cast at the foundry.

My large wooden meditation chair I designed out of rare, large-width sugar pine, with a slip-in dovetailed chair back design. Hand tooled. When Mary saw it first, she said it came from another dimension.

Ice.

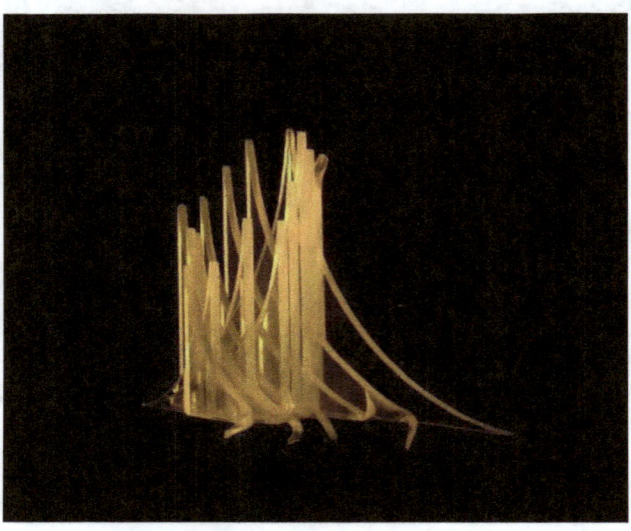

Catizone Cross. Heavy table-piece. Two perspectives of the same piece.

I made it in 4 sections using a lathe, milling machine, and finishing with a surface grinder with magnetic table/chuck for machining stability.

The tolerances: One-tenth of a thousandth. 0.0001 or one ten-thousandth. I measured it with light, using optical comparators. Then I silver-braised it together as one piece. The tolerances are so tight it appears to be made from one solid block of steel.

At the 3-family apartment building in North End that I made into a 4-family by adding a garret. You can see the large sugar pine meditation chair, and the multi axle hanging mobile.

Christy and Peter at a friend's outside art show.

Friends from Lake Como, Italy. Gianni, Peter, Renza and Christy.

Christy and Peter at Cafe North End.

Christy and Peter on her brother's boat heading to an Island on Cape Cod, Massachusetts.

Christy and Peter at Assembly Row.

Christy & Peter at Peter's nephew's wedding. Christy and Peter partying at a New York City restaurant, the night before   Tom Magliozzi (from Car Talk) son's wedding.

Christy, Peter, and our 240-pound English Mastiff, Benito, driving around North End, celebrating the Italians winning the Soccer World cup. Benito had been wearing his Italian flag bandana. His picture was in the Italian newspaper.

Christy and Benito.

Some images of our home, that I designed. The stained-glass window into the kitchen.

Adjusting a meditation bench in the kitchen, before shipping.

Since both levels of our home are an open floor plan, you can see the cherry column (which I had custom-made and flatbeded up from Pennsylvania) and the mahogany stairs and banisters from all areas of the house. I had the iron gates custom made as well.

Our bar. The tall cabinet to the right is my large humidor which holds 1,000+ cigars. I had to design the humidification system with special fans, placing hygrometer's throughout to measure the humidity. When I was done it held perfect humidity throughout.

Our Wolf commercial kitchen stove, which I call 'the Altar,'
maker of the Holy Eucharist.

Your host, in the kitchen.

The Bacchus Head was cast from a Bacchus head in Rome. At one point I
glued diamonds in his eyes and would occasionally glue a lit cigar in his
mouth!

Our wood burning fireplace, in the living room.

Having a cigar in the living room with our large 240 pound English Mastiff, Benito, (sticking his head out from under the coffee table) (I named him after Benito Mussolini.)

I built a copper base for our 3rd floor master bath jacuzzi.

The Easter piece.

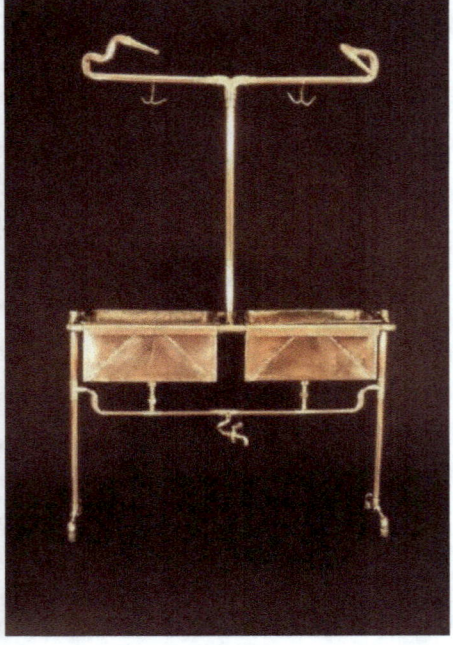

I designed and built this piece out of copper, brass, and steel for a popular restaurant in North End. I showed him the drawings and he accepted. But when I built it according to the drawings, I didn't like it. So I took it all apart and started from the beginning. Every night in my dreams I worked on it and when I woke up in the morning I knew exactly what I was going to do. When I walked through the plumbing supply store, I felt as if I was completing the design in real-time; I walked through the aisles intuitively knowing what to grab. I made my own copper sinks by building wooden forms first then molding the sheet copper to the wooden forms. I used an antique gas valve for draining the ice water.

It sat in their middle of their dining room where they hung fish, garlic, and salami from the horns and put clams and shrimp on ice in the bain-maries. It sat in my studio with the horns facing East as it would sit in the restaurant. I finished it at Easter and it perfectly symbolised the resurrection (the rising Sun facing East). Years later when the restaurant was moving, I bought it back for twice what I sold it for because the owner said, the price of copper went up! One of the waitresses told me customers loved it, and would ask what was it before. I took that as a big compliment because who can make something that looked like something it was before it was made?

Our espresso machine came from a café in Paris.

Our guestroom.

Our 180-pound Brindle English Mastiff, Lorenzo, taking a nap in our master bedroom on the 3rd floor and our movie theater & TV that disappears into the ceiling, which has great definition at night. When Tweeter (no longer in business) came in to install it, I told the manager we weren't going to build a sofit for the screen to disappear into, we were going to remove a section of the ceiling and have it disappear between the rafters. They said, "We have never done that before…" So I said, "We're going to do it today!"

Piano Noble, meaning Royal Floor in the Early Renaissance.

This view is from our second floor stairway up to the master bedroom. I designed and built a glass floor you can walk out on that's cantilevered into the cathedral ceilings of our master bedroom.

Living room library.

An almost panoramic view of the second floor.

Our coconut grove (the patio) and full view of our kitchen. There used to be an attic above which I removed and replaced with six skylights, so now you need sunglasses and a cigar to cook!

When you walk up from the street to our first floor your greeted by a large bottle neck palm tree.   Living room, hallway 2nd floor.

Dining room to living room view to library.

Always happy entertaining.

As usual, Tom and Peter smoking cigars at the Cafe Paradiso (now closed) in Harvard Square, Cambridge, MA.

Peter, Tom, and Ray looking at Barry's car engine in Harvard Square.

'Amish' (Jesse Esh) Peter and Tom at my house. Jesse Esh may have been the first Amish to have been driven to Boston—in this case to visit me—he was manufacturing meditation benches for me at the time.

Tom and Peter, smoking cigars at the Cafe Paradiso again. Years prior, Tom and Ray bought me a violin case (as a joke because I own guns) for my birthday. On this particular day I filled the violin case with loaded guns. That's why Tommy's laughing so hard.

We were all staying at the Savoy hotel in South Beach Miami when I took this picture.

Tommy and Peter smoking cigars in Harvard Square.

In New York at Tommy's son's wedding. On the big day, I embarrassed myself... When they told us we had to take pictures with the bride (Megan), I held both our cigars while Tom kissed the bride. When I bent over to kiss the bride, there was a flash of light and a scream... I had burnt a large hole in Megan's wedding veil. or the first time in my life, I understood the true Christian meaning of confession. I found myself telling everyone to purge me of my wicked sin, while I looked for the tallest building to jump off!

Sarah.

Joanna.

Peter with Ariel.

Ariel.

Cape Cod - Trying to make the best of my Republican in-laws.

A killer night with OJ Simpson at Smith & Wollensky's in South Beach, Miami!

My nephew's wedding. Waiting in the ER for my legendary emergency doctor friend we could have a drink and cigar.

Just finished a 2-week water-only fast and moved and walked in contemplative thought.

Waiting for a friend.

Our English Mastiff passed away, eventually we got a BRT Black Russian Terrier who was cheerful you wanted to kill him!

In the mood to paint.

PART III

WALKING ON WATER WITH A CIGAR

CHAPTER 14

<u>The Genius From America</u>

"Creation isn't about planning - it's about catching lightning in a bottle"

I was at a family gathering with Mary, and ended up talking to her brother-in-law, who was a Harvard business guy. I would have been about 30 years old at the time. Mary's sister's husband had all the credentials, but nothing ever seemed to work for him; he was a complete failure. He introduced me to one of his contacts, a man from India named Shiv Baid, with whom he had been doing some business. Little did he know that Shiv and I would end up doing an even bigger business deal...

I found out that Shiv's family had been in the diamond-cutting and polishing business in Bombay for generations. I knew nothing about diamonds and didn't particularly want to know anything—they seemed like a world away from my world of artistry and spiritual investigation—but there was effectively a sale on diamonds, and it seemed like a good deal. You know how it is, when there's a sale on pants, you buy pants. In this case, the sale happened to be on diamonds. So, just like that, I agreed to buy a shipment of diamonds.

If I remember right, the diamond consignment cost me around five or six thousand dollars. I'd made some money after buying and renovating my father's building, and letting out apartments, on top of my other artistic enterprises. Of course, there was more than a frisson of risk attached to the enterprise. There was the incipient fear that the diamonds could be intercepted or stolen en route, or might otherwise mysteriously disappear, or that I'd end up taking delivery of a shipment of worthless paste stones.

When the diamonds did finally, arrive safely, I still had no idea of what I was going to do with them. They were the real deal, at least.

Absolutely stunning. But I couldn't just revel in their beauty, somehow, I had to figure out what to do with them. Did you really think I had a business plan?! I never have a business plan. I've always put the cart before the horse, doing things on impulse. But I maintain that my naivety (or stupidity) is important because if I'd been a smart man, I'd never have bought the diamonds. In fact, I would never have done anything interesting with my life. I'd have overanalyzed every opportunity, got stuck in "analysis paralysis," and never achieved anything. I think it's so much better to just dive in and figure things out as I go.

So, there I was thinking, *Oh my God, What the hell am I doing with all these diamonds?* The Armenians, and the Jews had dominated the diamond market for centuries, what chance did a guy like me from North End have? I wasn't about to go into the diamond retail business, the last thing I wanted was a regular job... I wanted to *create* something. Admitting that to myself was the key. So, I did what I always did, I let the idea sit with me, I meditated on it, and I waited...

It's a funny thing, but when you have a shipment of diamonds just lying around, you stop thinking of them as a precious commodity. I wouldn't say I was using diamonds to score lines in my latest aluminium sculptures, but I stopped looking at them as priceless, untouchable things. I started playing with them, just seeing how the light played off their perfect-cut surfaces, seeing how they looked in different contexts. And one day, I stuck a diamond on my shoulder, just to see how it looked embedded against the skin. The skin held it in place for a moment, and then it fell. But before that diamond hit the floor, an idea was forming...

Suppose I could design and market a way to sell body-adhesive diamonds—wearable diamonds—as the ultimate fashion accessory. Back then, there was nothing like it.

This was way before the era of computers and cell phones, so I spent hours in libraries researching adhesives that had similar light refractive properties to the diamonds and could be safely applied to the skin. Eventually, I found a pressure-sensitive adhesive with a silicon-freon base that was sold in a downtown Boston store. It was originally used to glue toupees. At the time, I had a thick hairline, typical of a young Italian, so people probably thought I was buying all that toupee glue for myself. I was buying it by the case load.

I had a friend, Robert, who was a prim and proper retail businessman. He was so fascinated by my idea of wearable diamonds that he became my secretary. I told him I wanted to contact De Beers, and he said, "Forget it. They'll never talk to you unless you're doing $500 million in business."[26] That was like a red rag to a bull, and of course I called De Beers in New York straightaway. At the time, De Beers wasn't allowed to do business in the U.S., so they referred me to their brokers in Europe.

I called all five major brokers, and four of them told me, in no uncertain terms, to get lost. But one, Harry Stanfield, who was based in London, connected with me instantly. I didn't even have to sell him on the idea. He got it. He got *me*. We became fast friends. I even sent him one of the first cordless phones from the U.S., which he had modified for use in England.

With Harry's enthusiastic backing, things started to fall into place. I put the same energy and creativity into designing intricate and elegant arrangements to decorate the skin. The name: Body Roc came next (the missing 'k' seemed to highlight the softer, more ethereal nature of our new brand.) Ready to take over the world, I reached out to designers and fashionistas—what you might call influences nowadays—to share the concept. Harry loved the idea of Body Roc, but suggested it might work better with cubic zirconia, as people might be hesitant to wear diamonds for fear of losing them. He introduced me to a U.S.-based company in Michigan—the largest cubic zirconia manufacturer in the world.[27] International Crystal

---

[26] De Beers' control of the diamond market in the 1980s was estimated at 85% of global supply. U.S. antitrust laws prevented De Beers from direct operation in America, necessitating complex international business arrangements.

[27] Cubic Zirconia emerged as a major diamond alternative in the late 1970s. ICT was among the first companies to perfect the skull-crucible method of growing synthetic crystals, a process developed by Soviet scientists in the 1960s.

Technology (ICT) had divisions across Asia and worked with the U.S. government, developing crystals for space communications. They even grew emeralds and rubies from seeds.

Harry told me to tell ICT president Larry King I was a friend, and I spent a week pestering ICT, before Larry finally took my call. When we spoke, it was like magic. We talked for hours, and he invited me to Michigan to stay at his house. That weekend, I flew out, and we hit it off immediately. Larry was a brilliant man with graduate degrees in mechanical, electrical, and chemical engineering. He had a massive lab filled with giant computers, huge copper shafts descending into molten solutions, all controlled electrically. They would start with a tiny seed of a real ruby or emerald, attaching it to the bottom of the copper shaft. This shaft would turn so slowly you couldn't even see it move, but after hours you'd come back, and the seed would have grown into a full synthetic ruby or emerald.

Larry and his partner didn't just love my idea, they loved me too. In those days, I was handsome, smart, and brim-full of charisma. It would have been easy for people to think I had them all fooled, but people believed in me, and my confidence seemed to carry the whole thing forwards. We formed a corporation on the spot. Everything seemed to align perfectly. The connections, the timing, and the strange sense of déjà vu made it feel like I was picking up where I'd left off with these partners from a past life. Sometimes I even wondered if we had been working on crystals together in Atlantis.

They invested $30,000 in packaging, and I designed an equilateral triangular box with Italian colors, featuring a graphic of a woman's shoulder, a diamond, and adhesive. We decided on a three-tier distribution[28] system through jewelry stores, but I felt we needed to go further, targeting television and MTV to showcase the product. I

---

[28] The three-tier distribution system, commonly used in jewelry retail, consists of manufacturers selling to wholesale distributors, who then supply retail jewelry stores, which ultimately sell to end consumers. This traditional model enables each tier to focus on its specialized role: production, regional distribution, and customer-facing sales respectively.

envisioned a glamorous model on a rotating platform, with light-revealing diamonds on her skin—first one, then two, then three stones as the light brightened. The dramatic effect would captivate audiences. Larry and his team were hesitant, they were old-school and made their money through traditional distribution channels and advertising. But I was already making waves. *USA Today* ran an article on me, and *Boston Magazine* picked it up too. I contacted a prominent Boston fashion designer, Yolanda, and decorated her models with Body Roc. We aired some TV ads and viewers were enraptured; they'd never seen anything quite like it.

I slipped seamlessly into this new world of big business deals, and Mary saw me in a completely new light. Before that, she'd only ever seen me as some sort of funky artist with a philosophical background. She'd mentally placed me in that little box, with my spiritual leanings, my sculpture and ceramics, and then, all of a sudden, I was creating an empire out of nowhere, flying off to London with De Beers, and setting up manufacturing with ICT.

She must have wondered, *Where is this coming from?* I didn't have a background in business. My only experience was being creative—and being stupid. And I say that advisedly because, as I said, my stupidity was absolutely essential to my success. No matter the stakes or the pressure, I treated it all as just another form of performing art. I was really just having fun, playing in an unfamiliar world, and seeing how far I could take my outlandish ideas.

I knew I needed a good lawyer. A friend referred me to Michael West, a "lawyer's lawyer," highly respected in Boston. I offered him a 10% stake in the business in exchange for his legal services. He confirmed what I had already suspected: the idea wasn't patentable. That only made me more determined to partner with someone who could produce cubic zirconia in massive quantities to ensure market dominance. We needed product and we needed it to be accessible and affordable to millions.

I was on the phone with Larry Kelly at ICT, still trying to figure out how to solve the issue of the applicator. Looking every inch the diamond mogul, lounging on my chaise, speaking on my new cordless phone, cigar in hand, we were talking over our options. I was looking out over the dome of the Franciscan monastery with its giant cross, and further off, the dome of St. Stephen's, my church of transformation, and Larry was telling me he wanted to spend $30,000 to create an applicator. I told him to wait a moment, while I gave it some thought.

I got off the phone, lay back and emptied my head. I had learned to trust in my ability to conjure up answers out of cigar smoke and dreams. Sure enough, I had a vision of a small wooden dowel, just a couple of inches long. The adhesive we'd been using was pressure-sensitive, so I reasoned that we could put a tiny amount on the top of the dowel. Then, we'd take the stone—in this case, a cubic zirconia—touch its crown to the adhesive, and lift it up. The stone would sit perfectly on the dowel, like a pyramid.

This setup would allow us to apply adhesive to the pavilion of the stone, press it onto the skin, and twist. The whole thing would cost us one-third of a cent per applicator. I explained it all to Larry, and it was dead silent on the other end of the line. I thought we'd been disconnected. Then he said, "I've got to stop smiling before I can talk." Here's a guy with a deep background in engineering, and I had none. Yet, this ridiculously simple idea solved the problem, and sure enough, we rolled ahead with this as our applicator.

Harry Stanfield, my De Beers contact in London, introduced me to Milos Vainer, one of the top diamond brokers in Europe. Milos was fascinated by the concept and saw potential in using "brown goods"—diamonds from the Argyle mines in Australia that were too good to be used as industrial diamonds but not high enough quality for jewelry.

The full cost for five or six small cubic zirconia stones, the adhesive, the applicator, and all the packaging—including the graphics—was just 99 cents. That gave us plenty of room for profit. On Milos's suggestion, I then designed a cheaper version, using the Australian crystals, which we could sell for $9.95 instead of $19.95. It was all set up perfectly for a three-tier marketing strategy.

Milos invited me to stay at his home in Surrey. Harry and his wife, Beryl, picked me up from the airport. Beryl was an incredibly sharp Jewish woman who seemed to be the brains behind his operation in

London. Harry was absolutely nuts behind the wheel. Driving on the wrong side of the road was unsettling enough, but Harry's style of driving made it a heart-stopping experience. I thought, "This is how it ends. I survive all these risks in business, only to die in a car crash in London." But somehow, we made it.

Harry and Beryl had warned me about Milos's wife before we arrived. "She hates everyone," they said. "Don't take it personally." But when we met, it was the opposite—she treated me like her long-lost lover. She and her maid prepared endless meals, course after course, making me feel like royalty. It was a strange, surreal experience.[29]

I took my cubic zirconia samples with me to London and we exchanged stones. Milos showed me his exquisite pink diamond collection worth millions of dollars, and I handed him a pink cubic zirconia, worth about $15 wholesale. He looked at it under his loupe and said, "I cannot tell the difference between this and my pink diamonds." It wasn't until he looked at it with an electronic device that he was able to determine it was an imitation. He asked if he could buy it from me, but I gave it to him as a gift. He marveled at it, and aware of the sacrilege in one so intimately associated with the diamond trade said, "Why would anybody buy diamonds when these

---

[29] The Milos's home was an incredible place, and I was in good company. His tennis partner and close friend, Martina Navratilova, often stayed at his place. I ended up sleeping in the same bed she had used—though not at the same time, of course! Their son, Peter, was close friends with John Cleese's daughter. I heard stories about Cleese, including one about him being arrested for fighting with his wife on the streets of London. It made sense to me—anyone with his kind of humor must be borderline insane. His intensity was written all over his work, especially *Fawlty Towers*. Peter said they once asked Cleese to do something funny during lunch, and all he did was give them a particular look. They were rolling on the floor laughing—he didn't even have to say a word. It was surreal to hear stories about their luminous friends, and it all added to the feeling that I'd somehow landed in another world.

exist?"

Milos was in love with the idea of Body Roc, and introduced me to galleries, high-end jewelers, and distributors across London. He introduced me as "the genius from America," which felt absurd. But the simplicity of the idea combined with its marketability seemed to impress everyone. By then, I had already formed manufacturing partnerships in Michigan, so my focus was on establishing distribution across Europe and South America.

We were moving fast, but when I got back to Michigan, Larry Kelly suggested that the diamond industry wasn't able to move quite as quickly; they explained that diamond people didn't understand cubic zirconia back then. He told me stories about merchants coming out of New York with briefcases full of cash, paying top dollar for cubic zirconia because they didn't realize it wasn't a diamond. Milos himself had proven that even he couldn't tell the difference without subjecting it to very close scrutiny.

I formed the corporation with De Beers to handle all of Europe and South America. Milos's network was invaluable. His building in London was stunning, and he was cutting diamonds for the Queen and wealthy Arab clients. I worked with his team on designs using cubic zirconia to be followed by the Australian brown goods. His secretary, a stunning Black woman, became the model for testing designs in the office. It was surreal, working in this glamorous building and being treated as if I'd always belonged there.

It struck me that I was still sculpting, but instead of working with wood, metal, and glass, I was working with people and places. I was creating a new artform, arranging people and networks like materials to build something entirely new. Somehow, it all came together, despite my lack of experience. People had told me De Beers wouldn't even speak to me, yet there I was, setting up international distribution and working with some of the biggest names in the industry. I didn't have a business plan—I never did. But the power of stupidity kept me moving forward. I kept on walking out on stage and winging it. Sometimes, that's all it takes.

Then I was asked to give three lectures at the University of Miami. Don't ask me how I made the connection with Karen Barcello, the professor of marketing there. Sometimes things happen for unknowable reasons. It's like walking through the woods, figuring out your way instinctively, and then finding hidden paths among the trees that take you where you need to go via the scenic route.

Karen had heard about what I was doing and thought it would be a great case study for her students. I ended up giving three back-to-back lectures, each to 160 students. That's 480 students in total, all in one day. I hadn't prepared at all—what did I have to teach? When I got there, I decided to start each lecture by asking, "Are there any questions?" That got a laugh, and once everyone started laughing, we bonded, and the process began.

The lectures were a blast. They turned into another kind of performance art. I shared how Body Roc came to be and how it all evolved. It may not have been teaching per se, but I was able to give the students something else: insight into a process that was still unfolding, an awareness of the risks and pitfalls along the way, and best of all, an understanding of the simplest fact of business: that one good idea is the greatest commodity of all.

I came to appreciate how information is really just a catalyst for something greater to unfold. We put too much importance on information itself, but it's really just an excuse for teachers and students to get together and talk through ideas. Like people sometimes say about Moses parting the sea: *that's not so special, that kind of natural occurrence happens every now and then*, but they're missing the point; the fact that he was there when it happened is what gives it meaning.

The students got involved, and we even created small marketing displays together. Karen loved it. Her husband, Lou, and I became friends, and she proposed working on another project together in Miami. I adored the off-scriptedness of it all, and it felt like a magic trick unfolding. The trick was in having the idea, and building it up into a business, and I took an even greater joy in demystifying the process and sharing how it had all been done.

To misquote John Lennon, Body Roc was the perfect illustration of life happening because I'd actively decided against making other plans. If I'd ever settle down and got a 'proper' job, none of it would have occurred. I loved just going along for the ride, following all the ups and downs stoically, simply observing how each event influenced the next, never worrying about the bad things that happened, never getting too carried away with the good things.

If there was a moment that summed it all up—an apotheosis moment—it was when I was smoking cigars with a doctor friend. Suddenly I said, "I have to go." He asked, "Where are you going?" I replied, "I don't know, but I have to be on Newbury Street." I didn't know why, but I just knew I had to be there. When I arrived, all the local TV channels—Channel 4, Channel 5, Channel 7—were there with their cameras, and I ended up all over the news.

In retrospect, I can see that's how my life had always worked. Even as a kid, my mother had to put a harness on me during walks because, otherwise, I'd disappear into crowds. When I was in Catholic school, she'd drop me off in the hallway, but I wouldn't go to class. I'd wander off to Hanover Street and sit in cafes interacting with the men as they smoked and drank their espresso. I sought them out, almost as if that way of being was in my DNA from a former life.

Meanwhile, I made another useful contact, quite by chance... I decided sing in a Catholic church choir in Miami, which consisted of lawyers and their wives. Of course, I told them about Body Roc, and they said, "You have to meet our friend Micheal, he owns a radio station, and is president of the chamber of commerce in Miami." I called him, we had lunch, and I told him about Body Roc. Micheal said, "You don't know who I am, do you?" I confessed that I didn't. He told me, "I was the money behind the Mood Ring," which had been wildly successful. The coincidence of finding Micheal like that felt inspiring. Micheal was from an old banking family in Michigan, and loved the idea of Body Roc for the high-end market. He decided to do a deal with Karen and I, and It was another big step along the way. But we still needed something else to help us get noticed and I carried on riding that wave of good fortune...

I was living in North Beach and decided to walk down to South Beach, to First Street. While I was down there, I came across a new nightclub being built, and I met the designer. She traveled all over the world designing clubs, and we got talking. Naturally, since I'm like a walking, talking robot when I have an idea, I started telling her about Body Roc.

She said, "I have this friend, Cynthia Kay, who used to be Miss Chicago. She's a playmate who worked her way up the corporate ladder and is now one of the CEOs at *Playboy*. She's coming down here for a photo shoot in Coconut Grove, and I think she'd love this idea." With typical Catizone charm, I was able to persuade Cynthia to squeeze in an additional session for Body Roc, and she agreed.

We got together, and I ended up applying the stones all over her body for the shoot. It was an interesting experience because, for her, it was all very matter-of-fact. She was completely comfortable being naked—it was just another day at the office. For me, though, it was a bit surreal. There were some parts of her body that were particularly tricky to get the stones to adhere to properly, especially with the pavilion placement. Those silicone tits were particularly resistant. As they say, it was a dirty job, but someone had to do it! The nightclub designer who had introduced us was there as well. I could sense she had some interest in me, but I wasn't interested in opening that door. I was focused on the work and getting everything just right. *Playboy* liked the concept so much they decided to move forward with a major shoot featuring a blonde on black satin sheets, with stones placed all over her body. I ended up designing the layout for that shoot as well.

I was working on new ideas with Yolanda to incorporate Body Roc into clothing designs with special cut-out sections so the stones could be adhered to the skin. De Beers were getting excited about the possibility of expanding into the South American market. There were opportunities to pivot into the new age market, using different stones for chakras and healing along the spine. And I was pursuing more projects with Karen Barcello in Miami. Innovative new ideas were sparking off each other, and it felt as if we were on the cusp of something very big.

All of that good energy was addictive. I'm reminded of the giant wooden multi-axial sphere I built that hung from my ceiling. When the elements all aligned, I felt like the energy flowed perfectly. That's how I felt about Body Roc: everything just fell into place. It was like Jason waiting for the winds to come, sacrificing Iphigenia to set sail.

Everything lined up, but the tragic wisdom of ancient Greece loomed: *never do a woman wrong.* Was I about to fly too close to the sun?

Around that time, Rocco, an old friend from the North End, got involved. Rocco was a marketing genius who had started a company called Great Northern Swing out of a hole in the wall and turned it into a multimillion-dollar enterprise within a year. He was excited about the Body Roc idea and wanted to help. He even put together a focus group of marketing experts to workshop the concept. He spent several thousand dollars on this meeting, and the feedback was overwhelmingly positive. Everyone thought it was a winner.

I made friends with Manny Torti, a mechanical engineer and patent lawyer in Rhode Island. Rhode Island has this reputation for corruption—*deal with someone there, and you're probably dealing with gangsters.* At first, he dismissed the idea as ridiculous, but when he showed the packaging to his team at a marketing company, they were blown away. They told him, "Manny, this is brilliant. This could actually work." It was the kind of response I kept getting, no matter who saw the concept, they loved it. It was such a simple, stupid idea, but it resonated.

I never felt like I was running a business in the conventional sense—I was winging it. For me, it was never about learning the ins and outs of diamonds or becoming a gemologist. I didn't want to open a store or worry about grading stones. I was just happy taking an absurd idea— like sticking diamonds onto the skin—and seeing how far it could go.

After the preliminary had gone so well, I was due to fly out to Chicago or Atlanta for the full *Playboy* shoot. Around the same time, we got talking to Madonna's people about the possibility of her promoting the brand[30].

With word of mouth spreading, Body Roc was becoming a hot new look for those in the know. The problem was that without a patent and product on the shelves here-there-and-everywhere, it was just the preserve of the fashion magazines and a few select customers. It needed to be *everywhere*, but not enough people could actually go to

---

[30] Madonna went on to use the name "Body Rock" for a song,

155

the store and buy Body Roc for themselves.

Not only that, but the bigger the infrastructure behind Body Roc got, the more complicated the whole enterprise became. The beautiful simplicity of the idea was in danger of getting lost under layers of potential stakeholders. That phrase about finding diamonds in the rough comes to mind.

At some point, ICT sent the first shipment to London. One of Larry Kelly's managers in Michigan, who had fallen for a young sales clerk in a store, decided to use her on the packaging. They changed my original design, which was elegant, to something that looked like it belonged in a circus. When De Beers saw it, they hated it because it looked cheap and undermined the brand's image.

Milos was still in love with the idea and willing to go along with anything; but ICT was causing problems. They didn't want to do photo shoots, or investigate any more progressive strategies. They wanted to stick to their regular three-tier distribution system because that's how they made all their money. Too many of my traditionally-minded partners were too cautious and grounded, and were resistant to my wild leaps and more outré ideas. In a business that had been built the traditional way, I courted too much resistance with my unconventional, fast-moving approach.

As alliances deteriorated and confidence crumbled, I felt as if I was being squeezed out by certain parties. I felt as if I had no choice but to fly out to Northern Michigan, unannounced, to confront Larry Kelly and demand he hand over my shares and contracts on the spot. It was a risk of course. I could have ended up on a woodchipper and then you'd never be reading about any of this! When I told my mafia friend, Vinnie Di Gangi, that I was going to Michigan to 'take care of business,' he wanted to know if I was taking any muscle along for the ride. We both knew plenty of guys who could accurately be described as tough guys—the sort of guys whose head, neck and body appeared to be made of one piece. But I said I'd get along fine without them.

I walked into Larry's office, and his secretary, Denise, called to say I wanted to speak to him. There was a pause as Larry evidently suggested she should stall and say he'd call me back. That was when she had to interrupt, "Mr. Kelly, you misunderstand. Mr Catizone isn't on the phone, he's here now, waiting to see you."

When he came out to see me, Larry was as pale as a ghost. His wife, who clearly didn't like him, watched the encounter, and visibly seemed to relish the sight of him sweating buckets, with a Mona Lisa smile on her face. He was all charm and bluster and tried to demur any sort of settlement, but this North End veteran wasn't about to be schmoozed out of anything. I told him I wasn't leaving until I'd got what I came for, and he could see I meant it. He had no choice but to comply. It was sad that our relationship had to end that way.

On the flight back to Boston, as the plane struggled to land, I couldn't help but think about the irony: surviving that confrontation only to die in a plane crash would have felt like the ultimate pyrrhic victory. Thankfully, I made it back safely, but the experience solidified how fragile the whole enterprise had become.

After I got back, I told Vinnie, "What those guys didn't know was whether I was crazy, or I had balls the size of Michigan." And he said, "Peter, you are crazy! But you also have balls the size of Michigan!"

The biggest frustration about the collapse of Body Roc was simply that it didn't achieve everything it could have done. Everyone kept telling me how smart I was. Maybe it was because the idea was so simple, and everything just fit together so well that it made them wonder why no one else had thought of it. It was like the invention of the wheel: obvious in hindsight, but it took so long for early man to stop dragging things around! I'd had so many people believing in me, and my idea, and praising the concept, that I'd started to buy into the hype. I should have just relaxed and enjoyed the dance. Now, I often tell people, "Don't trust anyone who thinks you're smart!"

In spite of everything, it wasn't a disheartening experience. In retrospect, I can only perceive it as a blessing. Had it all succeeded, I might have become a terrible person, selfish, shallow, and less thoughtful. When my father died, I took on aspects of his personality: fancy cars, fancy clothes, and fancy women. On some unconscious level it felt like a way of keeping him alive. When my mother passed, I noticed myself becoming more aggressive, reflecting her own nature. If Body Roc had become wildly successful, I might have lost myself entirely.

Despite the collapse, the journey illuminated a deeper truth about creation. It wasn't just about the business; the whole endeavor was proof of my abiding sense of the Trinity—of thought, motion, and creation—working in beautiful accord. Like in Hinduism's three planes of consciousness, it all came together: the pure thought, the movement behind it, and the physical manifestation. It was co-creation, an expression of Divine energy channeled through human hands. The fact that Body Roc got off the ground at all, and that it intrigued and energized so many people was ultimately more fulfilling to me than any commercial success could have been.

Even as things unraveled, I could only focus on just how exhilarating the whole process had been. From forming partnerships with De Beers to doing a shoot with *Playboy*, every step felt like a surreal dance—one led by intuition and serendipity rather than logic. It might have all fallen apart in the end, but for a brief moment, I had wings, and I flew, albeit a little too close to the sun.

You might be wondering what happened to that consignment of diamonds I bought that kickstarted the whole adventure... After switching to stick-on cubic zirconia for the Body Roc concept, I ended up selling the diamonds wholesale since I no longer needed them. Because I'd purchased them at such a great deal, I was able to recoup my money. Fortunately, diamonds don't depreciate. When I sold them to people in the diamond business, they were baffled. "You did what? You formed a partnership with De Beers?" they'd ask, blown away. These were people running small brick-and-mortar operations, and here I was, some outsider who had gone straight to the top, skipping all the traditional steps. It was like *David and Goliath*. I had thrown the stone, hit the giant in the head, and knocked him out, giving myself just enough time to do my little dance. And then Goliath would have come around with a little cubic zirconia stuck to his temple!

CHAPTER 15

<u>Finding Balance</u>

"Sometimes the simplest design can unlock the deepest truths"

Mary and I stayed together through Body Roc and beyond, but over time, we drifted apart. In the first half of our relationship, I was fully committed to being monogamous. I had opportunities to stray, but I never acted on them. Then I discovered that Mary was having an affair with one of her colleagues at the Art Institute of Boston.

I'd sensed something was amiss for a long time, but whenever I brought it up, we would just talk in circles. Mary was so intellectually brilliant, and so well trained in argument, there was no way to pin her down. One day, I told her something I'd read—it may have been from Plato—that "truth is the handmaiden to lies."[31] The moment I said it, she turned white. It was as if she realized then that I understood that truth and lies were often intertwined and that no matter what she said, it wouldn't change what I knew. From that moment, she couldn't control the narrative with her words or her evasion.

Ironically, it wasn't Mary who finally told me the full truth, it was the man she was having the affair with. When he confirmed my suspicions, I calmly suggested to Mary that we split up. There was no acrimony; I was just keen that we didn't waste the time we had to get out there and find other people to fall in love with. But Mary didn't want to part, so we stayed together a little longer, although our

---

[31] As truth is the handmaiden to lies, so truth without love can be persecution. St. Paul persecuted the Christians. Then he found God and became a disciple of truth out of fear, only to continue his persecution of the Christians. Because without love, truth can be a falsehood.

relationship shifted. We lived in the same house and maintained a relationship, but I was no longer committed to monogamy. I started seeing other people, and we simply coexisted until we finally put our lost love out of its misery.

Our relationship lasted eighteen transformative years, where I bridged the worlds of art and academia, mixing the intellectual with the unconventional. During that time, I was surrounded by a whole array of different friends and groups. It was a Renaissance period for me, spanning my evolution from street-smart artist to someone who could navigate both intellectual and business worlds. But even as I changed and grew, something remained constant—that ability to see the Divine in the ordinary, to find meaning in the intersection of different worlds.

After Body Roc collapsed, I turned my attention to something that might conventionally be described as more meaningful: designing meditation benches. I was invited to a Buddhist meditation in Cambridge and saw a bench used for the seiza position[32]. It had a fixed angle that wasn't ideal for everyone, so I redesigned it. I rounded the leg base, making it more ergonomic so it adjusted to the sitter's body. I designed and added a spring cam system hinge, allowing it to fold for portability. This made it perfect for travel. I even created lightweight versions for people trekking in Tibet.

I sold a few benches, and word got around. More and more orders came in from all over the country... and then all over the world. The feedback was incredible, hundreds of testimonials from people who said they simply hadn't been able to meditate before using my bench. It found its way into monasteries worldwide, from strict Orthodox Christian communities to Sufi circles in the Middle East. One Buddhist

---

[32] The seiza position, a traditional Japanese formal sitting posture where one kneels with the buttocks resting on the heels, has been adapted for Western practitioners through the use of meditation benches (seiza benches and then my Omni Meditation Benches). The benches are designed to reduce the pressure on the ankles and knees by elevating the buttocks, and that enables to user to meditate in greater comfort for longer.

abbot in Chicago ordered benches for all his students. The Omni Bench became a quiet success, providing spiritual benefit to people worldwide. You can read some of my Testimonials in Appendix 2.

The design evolved through necessity and inspiration. While the spring cam hinge worked, it was expensive—$10 per hinge. I spent a month trying to find a cheaper solution. Finally, I meditated for two hours, and in a moment of clarity, I envisioned a hammer smashing the hinge. The answer was friction. I replaced the spring and cam system with a process called "staking," creating friction in the hinge knuckles. This reduced the cost to $1 per hinge and even solved safety issues, as people had caught their fingers in the original design.

Finding the right hinge was a challenge. I spent over $1,000 calling manufacturers in China, only to discover it didn't exist. The hinge became unique to my benches, and I refused to sell it to competitors. However, manufacturing at scale came with its own drama. I landed a major wholesale account before I had the machinery to fulfil it. I subcontracted a machinist, but he disappeared with my stock. Desperate, I involved the police, tracked him down, and confronted him at his shop.

He wouldn't let me in, claiming he lacked insurance. That wasn't going to stop a Catizone in full flight, so I forced my way inside and told him, "You're getting on a machine, and I'm getting on a machine, and we're doing this now." I was determined not to lose the account. Together, we pushed out the hinges. It was a wild experience, but when you're younger, you do whatever crazy thing it takes to make something work.

I had a wonderful run with the meditation bench, and I often joked that, like the Catholic church, I made plenty of money in the religious business. The years passed, and I carried on handcrafting benches for people all over the world, helping people to meditate without pain, and opening them up to more rewarding meditative experiences.

Over time, more and more people copied the design, and a patent is only as good as your pockets are deep. Even after I found I could get the product manufactured in the Midwest and Canada, the production costs continued to rise and with more and more copycats out there, my market share shrank. I considered manufacturing in

China, but I didn't know if it was the right move. After 40-years in production, I'd set things up so that the business pretty much ran itself, but the question remained as to whether I should fight to keep it alive.

I went to bed thinking about it and had a dream. In the dream, I was smoking a cigar, flicking ashes into an ashtray made out of a stuffed iguana. As I thought about the idea, wondering whether it was dead or worth pursuing, I noticed the iguana had a pulse in the neck—it was alive. That gave me the resolve I needed, the idea wasn't dead. The next day, I decided to move forward with manufacturing in China, and it turned out to be the right decision. That dream showed me the way.

The Omni Bench felt like more than just a product—it was a bridge between East and West, between comfort and spirituality. It helped people find their way to meditation, just as I had found my way through various spiritual practices. In the end, it wasn't about the money or success; it was about creating something that helped people on their own spiritual journeys.

I realized that sometimes the simplest solutions are the most profound. Just as the bench helped people find physical balance in meditation, it helped me find balance between my creative drive and spiritual aspirations. It wasn't about chasing millions; it was about sustainable success that aligned with my deeper values.

The business kept growing, quietly and steadily, much like a meditation practice itself. Each bench that went out into the world carried a piece of what I'd learned about balance, about finding the middle way between ambition and contentment, between material success and spiritual growth.

CHAPTER 16

Full Circle

"Life is theater, and every guest deserves a good show"

I was living in Cambridge with a lady called Nancy, who was a lawyer. Nancy did everything for me. She cooked amazing dinners, had lived in Paris, and was beautiful. She even worked on my legal issues in the mornings before heading to work. The sex was great, too. Everything about her was perfect... except she was just too nice. Somehow, I couldn't cope with that.

We decided to part ways. Nancy was simply too nice. On some level, I was always looking for a woman that reminded me of my mother. Someone with a bit more spice...

I had a business address in Harvard Square, Cambridge. It was just a PO box, but I often walked by a place called The Harvest. The restaurant had recently been bought by Grill 23, a high-end steakhouse in Boston where people could spend $30,000 on lunch without batting an eyelid. They'd poured a million or more into renovating The Harvest, turning it into a sleek, upscale spot popular with dignitaries, intellectuals, and government officials.[33]

The restaurant had a stunning patio and exuded sophistication. They hired a woman by the name of Christy to manage the front of the house. One day, as I walked by, I saw her. To be completely honest, it was total lust at first sight. She was beautiful, always moving with a kind of organized chaos, managing the place with unflappable calm. For a year, I walked past without stopping—admiring her from a

---

[33] The Harvest Restaurant, opened in 1975, became a landmark of Harvard Square's transformation from bohemian enclave to upscale dining destination. The restaurant was known for bringing French culinary techniques to New England ingredients.

distance but never approaching. I didn't want to be regarded as a "Peeping Peter," after all.

Then one day, I saw her walking outside. I was driving into the square and, determined to keep her in sight, I made an illegal U-turn in front of a line of trucks. Horns were blaring, but I didn't care. I found out later that she remembered that day, too—mainly because she thought, *who's the asshole cutting across traffic?*

Later, my friends, the Van Vactors, suggested we meet for lunch at The Harvest. Pat was teaching at the Sorbonne at the time, and they often stayed in Paris, but when they were back, we always caught up. During lunch, Christy came to our table. I looked her straight in the eye and said, "You're the most beautiful woman in Cambridge." She smiled and replied, "You should come in more often!"

Sometime after, I noticed the restaurant was empty one morning. Christy was doing bookkeeping at the bar. The door was unlocked, so I walked in and handed her my card. I could tell by the way she took it in her hand and studied it that there was mutual interest. "Okay," she said, "I'll call you sometime."

Valentine's Day rolled around, and to my surprise, she did call. She agreed to go on a date but added, "I have a French boyfriend who's in Europe on business." To me, that sounded like her exit plan, she didn't know who I was, after all, and was hedging her bets. She checked her schedule and said, "The only day I have free is the day I'm getting a root canal."

I laughed, "You've got to be kidding. You're going to be drooling!"

"It's either that," she said, "or wait another month."

So, I took it. I picked her up from the dentist with a bouquet of flowers, dodging cars and honking horns to get there on time.

We walked through North End, where I introduced her to some of the locals. That's when we ran into my old friend Lobo, and she could tell, just by his presence, that he was a hitman. And we bumped into Danny Popolo. "Danny," I said, "last I heard, you took a bullet to the head!" Christy looked on as Danny said, matter-of-factly, "Nah, it just grazed me. They tried to whack me at Café dello Sport, but they didn't succeed." That helped set the tone for our whirlwind romance.

Christy lived in a small room in Newton, like a Genoese spinster. Genoese are known for their frugality, they're even called the Italian Jews. There's a saying that it takes seven Jews to equal one Genoese. She came from an impressive lineage herself. Her grandfather, Judge Francesco (Frank) Laveroni was born in Genoa in 1879, and was one of the first Italians to attend Harvard and went on to become the youngest appointed Judge in the United States at the age of 29. In addition to his judicial duties, he worked as a lawyer, you could carry out both roles at the time. He also founded St. Michael's Cemetery for Italian Catholic burials—where my parents are buried.

Judge Leveroni was knighted twice by the King of Italy, and wrote and passed legislation pertaining not just to Italian immigrants, but to immigrants entering the US from around the world. He was friends and worked with the then President, Calvin Coolidge, and together, they passed child labor laws to help protect children wandering the streets. He's widely known throughout the Boston area for founding the Home for Italian Children in Jamaica Plain, Massachusetts, an institution that survives to this day. (Once a year my family would shut our restaurant doors and donate our time and food to feed "The Home for Italian Children.") I could never have imagined I would eventually marry the Granddaughter of the founder. (Christy's mother's side of the family in Georgetown, Washington DC are all judges and lawyers.)

It gets wilder; I'm sure you'll have heard about the Ponzi Scheme[34], well it was Charles Ponzi who helped legitimize himself by doing business with Judge Leveroni, who also founded Leveroni Financial, which Christy's brothers now run.

Judge Leveroni was also a close friend of Isabella Stewart Gardner who founded the world-famous Isabella Stewart Gardner Museum in Boston. The Judge worked with officials in Italy to import a great many of the art works to the Museum. Now, almost every tourist that comes to Boston visits that museum (most of our guests do.) Some years ago, when Christy and her sister were visiting St Anthony's church in the North End, they met two old Italian ladies at the church. When they told them their grandfather was Judge Franceso Leveroni, the old ladies got on their knees and made the sign of the cross.

I love those little synchronicities in life, and I'm always looking out for them in my own life experience...

About a year before I'd met Christy, I'd been shopping in Chinatown with my French daughter, Joanna. We went into a very nice store, and I saw this absolutely gorgeous two-piece woman's dress, so ornate and beautifully embroidered I bought it. I also bought a ring. Joanna

---

[34] Charles Ponzi (1882-1949) created what became known as the "Ponzi scheme" - a type of fraud where returns are paid to earlier investors using funds obtained from later investors, creating the illusion of a profitable enterprise. In 1920, Ponzi's scheme in Boston promised 50% returns in 45 days by supposedly arbitraging international postal reply coupons. By associating with respected figures like Judge Leveroni and conducting legitimate business through Leveroni Financial, Ponzi initially gained credibility in Boston's Italian-American community. However, his scheme ultimately collapsed, costing investors millions of dollars. The term "Ponzi scheme" has since become synonymous with this type of investment fraud. His connection to Judge Leveroni's legitimate financial institution demonstrates how fraudsters often seek to build trust by associating with respected community figures. This was particularly effective in tight-knit immigrant communities where trust networks were crucial for business relationships.

asked, "Who are those for?" I had no idea at the time, but later I understood that they were waiting for Christy.

On one of our earliest dates, Christy gave me a warning during dinner. She said, "I'm a guy on the inside, a woman on the outside." I replied, "Perfect! I'm a guy on the outside, and a woman on the inside. I've been a lesbian my whole life and gotten away with murder!" Actually, my friend Rocco who helped with marketing Body Roc, once took me to see a woman who did automatic writing—where she writes without looking, supposedly channeling past lives and hidden truths. She told us that Rocco and I had been gay lovers and ran a little antique shop in Paris at the turn of the century. When she said it, I laughed and said, "That's the farthest thing from me—I might be a lesbian, but I'm not gay!" It became a joke between Rocco and me. She'd even told us our names in that life: I was Maurice, and he was Bruno. We'd tease each other about who was on the bottom.

My relationship with Christy moved quickly. *Very* quickly. This was despite the fact that she was still in touch with her French boyfriend, Alain. I didn't see it as much of a challenge. "An Italian versus a Frenchman?" I thought. "Piece of cake." We were married within three weeks of our first date. When Alain returned and Christy told him, "I'm married," he was understandably shocked and sarcastically asked, "Who did you marry? Guido from the North End?"

Why did we marry so quickly? It wasn't just my out-of-control lust at play. On some level, it felt like a recapitulation of previous events. My mother and father were Christy and Peter, and I had been searching for someone who evoked something of my mother; not her cruelty, but her edge, I think. Her feistiness. Her uncompromising uniqueness. I had been looking for someone who would surprise me, and keep me on my toes. Christy gave me all of that, and more, and I knew we should get married.

Her reason for marrying me? Christy said I reminded her of her father, a full-blooded Genoese. He was a striking man, who had married a beautiful Irish woman, and Christy was very close to him. We actually had two weddings. The first was with a justice of the peace in Cambridge. I hadn't been to confession in over 50 years, but the Justice of the Peace shrugged, gave us his blessing and said, "You're

167

good to go." We got married at a justice of the peace in Cambridge.

Then, to honor Christy's Irish Catholic mother's wishes, we had a full Catholic ceremony about a year later, in Cotuit, Cape Cod. It was a large full-blown traditional wedding, in a church with a Catholic priest, Father Toste, and relatives came from around the country. It was a beautiful summer day, and it was fully catered at the beautiful 5-acre Leveroni family estate, across from the ocean. Everything was cooked on the premises and served on grass lawns with large pitched white tents. There was a full bar, and the champagne flowed; it was a wonderful occasion.

In the 2010s, Christy and I purchased a building and started working on it with the aim of turning it into something... I didn't even bother getting an inspector in; it was perfectly obvious it all needed renovating and restoring, from the foundations to the roof. We took it on piecemeal, bit by bit. The building became our Airbnb venture. We only have one guest room, but it's been amazingly successful. I've been told that our listing got something like 50,000 hits in about two weeks.

Over the years, we've hosted all kinds of fascinating guests. We hosted an Australian guest, who had won the America's Cup; I didn't even know what the America's Cup was! A British guest who stayed with us said, "Peter, thank you. This is the first time my wife has smiled and laughed since our son was murdered in San Francisco." It was a poignant reminder of how humor and connection can bring people joy, even in their darkest moments.

The Airbnb is more than just a business, it's another stage for performance. It gives me a captive audience, and I make people laugh. It's like shooting fish in a barrel. Fortunately, Christy keeps me grounded. She often says, "Peter, these guests didn't come here to see you, they came to see Boston." She's right, of course, but I can't help holding them captive with stories, even when they'd rather be out exploring. I love an audience, and I thrive on those moments of connection.

I'll admit it. I am a tremendous narcissist. I told my wife that she has to donate my ego to Harvard when I die—they're gonna have to build an extension to take it, of course! This part of my life has always felt like a balancing act between ego and humility. I joke about being a narcissist; I love hearing myself talk, hearing myself sing. When you call me, it's my voice singing on the voicemail. Someone once said, "I can't believe you've got yourself singing on your voicemail!" But that's part of the creative process, isn't it? Most artists are narcissists. It's all about, "Look at me, look at what I've made." Life is theater, and creativity demands a performance. But as I hope you've realized, I temper my narcissism with my stupidity. It's an interesting mix that has made for an eventful life.

At this stage of life, I feel as if I've found a perfect balance. My Airbnb lets me perform, connect, and share stories, all while staying rooted in the neighborhood that shaped me. Even now, I think about the connections I've made and the crazy paths that led to them. Like when I'd meet someone at random, and suddenly, everything would click into place. That's the magic of living creatively—you never know where an idea or a chance meeting will take you...

When I was in Miami South Beach, I was supposed to be meeting my friends Tom and Ray (from *Car Talk*) for dinner, but instead of meeting them, I somehow ended up at Smith and Wollensky's; I'm not even sure how. As soon as I crossed the threshold, I saw him with his entourage at the bar... OJ Simpson – one of the most recognizable people in the United States at that time[35]. For some reason, he looked over, our eyes locked, and without knowing what was happening, we were walking towards each other. Spontaneously, we threw open our arms to hug each other, and we kissed like the dearest friends.

---

[35] Orenthal James "O.J." Simpson (1947-2024) was an NFL Hall of Fame running back who later became an actor and sports commentator. In 1994-95, he stood trial for the murders of his ex-wife Nicole Brown Simpson and her friend Ron Goldman in what became known as "the trial of the century." Though acquitted in criminal court, Simpson was later found liable in a civil trial and ordered to pay $33.5 million to the victims' families. In 2008, he was convicted of armed robbery and kidnapping in Las Vegas and served nearly nine years in prison before being released in 2017. OJ died from cancer on April 10, 2024 at age 76, leaving behind a complex legacy.

With the deepest kind of recognition in his eyes, he said, "How have you been?" And before we knew it, we were just carrying on as if we had known each other all our lives. I knew then that we must have known each other from another lifetime. We spent the entire evening together, drinking into the early morning. They were trying to close the place, but we just kept on talking, as if we were making up for lost time. He told me all about the trial, prefacing it by saying, "I don't talk to anyone about the trial anymore... but I feel compelled to tell you."

Impudent as ever, I stopped him at one point to ask, "Who did it?"

He simply said, "I know, but I can't say!"

I sensed the weight on his shoulders, and it was clear to me that he had been involved in some way, but whatever involvement he'd had, I felt immense empathy for him. To lift the mood, I told him about my concept for this very book, which he loved. He told me he knew a great literary agent in New York, but I didn't want to burden him anymore, so I said, "OJ, the most important thing in Italian Yoga is the moment we're in with our family and friends." He gave a huge sigh of relief and smiled, relaxing back into the moment.

OJ's girlfriend—another Christy—looked so much like his late wife, she could have been her twin. When I got up to go to the men's room, Christy got up to walk with me as far as the lady's room. Conspiratorially she turned to me and said, "You're hot!" I said, "I know!" She took my cell number.

You'll see a picture of me with OJ in the next group of photographs towards the end of the book. It was taken sometime in the wee, small hours, by which time I was drunk and half asleep. We parted in the same spirit as we'd met, and I never expected to hear from OJ again. But a couple of days later, I got a call from OJ's girlfriend Christy, saying "OJ really likes you and wants you to have his cell phone number. Just don't call him before eleven, he's playing golf."

I took my usual trip to the News Cafe (where Versace hung out; his people were from the same town in Calabria as my father's people). I called OJ at 11:30 am to suggest that he join me for lunch. He said that he'd love to, but that he had a meeting with his lawyers this afternoon. However, he told me he'd be going to Boston soon, because his daughter was at Boston University, and he'd call me when he arrived. I said he could stay in our guest room, and he was delighted. We carried on our conversation from where we'd left off the night before, exploring the deep connection we seemed to share.

Sadly, OJ never came to stay. Not long afterwards, he got arrested in Las Vegas, and ended up going to prison for 9 years. His cellphone was disconnected, and we never spoke again. When I landed back in Boston from Miami, I called my Christy to ask her to pick me up. When I told her I'd spent an evening with OJ Simpson, she wasn't too impressed, and told me to make my own way back! When I made it home, she'd deadbolted the doors and moved a piece of furniture to block off the master bedroom. It took me a whole year before I could tell her I'd invited OJ to stay with us but that she shouldn't worry... I would have hidden all the knives!

I love the spontaneity of chance meetings like that. Not long ago, I was walking down Hanover Street one time, with an investment banker I'd met randomly at a garage. Frankie, the Neapolitan restaurant owner, came out and said, "Peter's a legend." The banker turned to me and said, "You know, it's one thing to think you're a legend, but it's another when someone else says you are." Another time, Frankie asked me, "When did you retire? Wait—when did you ever work?" He wasn't wrong. I always made it look like I wasn't working. Whether I was on a rooftop or in a café, I somehow managed to make things happen. That's just my style.

It's funny how life comes full circle. Here I am, back in the heart of Boston, still telling stories, still making connections, still performing. The street kid from North End has become the host, welcoming people from around the world, sharing not just a room but a piece of his life, his humor, his wisdom. And maybe that's the biggest transformation of all: finding a way to turn every aspect of life into art, into performance, into connection.

Christy and I have created more than just a successful business, we've created a stage where every guest becomes part of our ongoing story. And isn't that what life is really about? Not just the big moments of transformation, but the daily acts of connection that remind us that we're all part of something larger than ourselves.

CHAPTER 17

The Trinity Revealed

"When thought, motion, and creation align, the Divine reveals itself in the ordinary"

It took me a weekend to figure out something profound: the universe has emotional intelligence. It's not part of the equations scientists use, and it's certainly absent from artificial intelligence, but emotional intelligence is essential; it's part of what makes us human.

As a Westerner, I came to understand this through the *Bhagavad Gita*. When Arjuna goes to war with his blood brothers, I realized it's not just a literal battle—it's a metaphor. The warrior saint Arjuna chose Krishna's wisdom rather than his armies, in turn winning the war against his blood brothers.

I always tell Hindu scholars: Arjuna wasn't going into war with his blood brothers, that's just a metaphor for going into war with himself. Arjuna was upholding his Dharma. They would ask, where did you read that? I said, in my heart. I call it emotional intelligence. (It should also be a part of a Cosmology equation, because the Universe is also emotional.)

I was on the beach, smoking a cigar, totally immersed in thinking about occasional erratic behaviors of the Universe and pondering the question of *why*. That's when I had my epiphany: The Universe has emotions!

The idea felt revolutionary to me. It's a reflection of how our feelings possess their own form of intelligence. Sometimes, when you're too immersed in something, as they were in their study of the *Bhagavad Gita*, you miss the deeper metaphorical layers. I keep going back to Henry Rousseau and my admiration for what he achieved with his primitive style; how he brought a fresh, unrefined perspective to his work. I feel like I'm a primitive thinker, offering that same raw insight.

So, what does it mean that the universe has emotional intelligence? Like us, the universe changes its behavior due to its emotional state and consciousness.

It means there's a symbiosis between thought, feeling, and creation. And that's the basis for my thoughts on the Trinity that I've been working towards my entire life. I've used that metaphor of the coal ovens before—like the ones in my family's Italian restaurant—they had a personality, and they were temperamental, so you had to feel your way intuitively through the cooking process. Was it too hot? You'd adjust the coals. Too cool? You'd feed it more. Maybe you'd toss a little water in. It required a relationship, an understanding. And while gas ovens were easier, coal ovens made better pizza, almost as if the story of the struggle, and the emotion of the journey was imprinted on the dough.

Cosmologists fail to understand this idea because emotions are not a part of their equation. In order to understand the Universe, we first have to understand ourselves. When asked, Einstein said he couldn't explain the relationship between his wife and first cousin/lover because it was too complicated (emotional).

Like scientists, I think the institutional church falls short in its disregard of the concept of emotional intelligence; they reduce everything to pure thought or doctrine. But emotion, that vital energy, is what animates understanding and creation. Without it, they're missing an essential element. It may not be something you can measure or quantify, but emotional intelligence is one of the forces that makes creativity, connection, and co-creation possible.

This interplay of emotion and creation has parallels everywhere. It's something I understand from my own work; whenever I create something, I experience a euphoric state. I ask myself: *What's the chemistry of those feelings?* And that's when it hit me: we're co-creators with the universe. The Trinity isn't about Father, Son, and Holy Ghost in a rigid sense. It's about *thought, motion, creation*.

Here's how it works: You think of a table—that's the thought. You go to the lumber yard to get the materials—that's the motion. You build the table—that's the creation. It's so simple, yet it's profound. That's the basis of the Trinity at work.

In Christian thought, this mirrors the Divine Trinity: God the Father as the eternal thought, the Holy Spirit as the Divine motion, and Christ the Word as the creative force through whom all things were made. "In the beginning was the Word," the Gospel of John tells us, suggesting that creation itself begins with Divine thought made manifest.

Consider how each element flows into the next, like a sacred dance—what Hindu tradition might recognize as the cosmic dance of Nataraja, Lord Shiva's creative movement that brings the universe into being. The thought comes first, in your mind's eye, you see the table. Perhaps it's a sturdy farmhouse piece, weathered oak with proud edges, or maybe it's sleek mahogany with curves that catch the light. This vision exists purely in the realm of imagination, perfect and complete, yet incorporeal, like Brahman, the ultimate reality beyond form.

Then comes the motion. Your feet carry you forward, your hands select the lumber. Each board you choose is an act of translation, moving your thought from the ideal into the physical world. The grain of the wood speaks to you, suggesting possibilities. This is like the Hindu concept of Shakti, the Divine energy that transforms potential into actuality. The weight of the materials in your arms reminds you that creation requires effort, requires movement through space and time—maya, the world of physical manifestation.

Finally, there's the creation itself—the making. Your hands guide the saw, the plane, the chisel. Sawdust fills the air like incense, marking this act as something ceremonial, like the Christian sacraments that make the Divine tangible in the material world. Each joint you fit, each surface you smooth, brings your original thought closer to physical reality. Yet what emerges is never quite the table you first imagined—it's something new, something that exists in dialogue between your initial vision and the properties of the materials themselves, much as the Christian concept of incarnation represents Divine perfection entering into dialogue with physical reality.

This Trinity repeats in all acts of making, reflecting what Hinduism calls the three gunas: sattva (thought, clarity), rajas (motion, activity), and tamas (material manifestation). The painter first sees the landscape in their mind, then moves to gather brushes and pigments, and finally creates the painting. The composer hears the melody in their thoughts, moves to the piano, and creates the score. The gardener dreams of roses, moves to prepare the soil, and creates the flower bed.

Each step is essential, each step transforms the one before it. The thought provides the spark—like the Christian concept of Divine Will or the Hindu concept of sankalpa (intentional consciousness). Without motion it remains ghostly and unfulfilled, like grace without works. The motion provides the bridge—the Holy Spirit's movement or Shakti's flow—but without both thought and creation, it's just aimless wandering. The creation provides the culmination, but without the thought and motion that preceded it, it would have no purpose, no soul.

This is how we participate in the act of creation, through this sacred Trinity of thought, motion, and making. In Christian terms, we are made in the image of a Creator God, and our creative acts echo the Divine creation. In Hindu understanding, we participate in the continuous unfolding of the universe, the eternal dance of creation (srishti), preservation (sthiti), and dissolution (pralaya). It's a pattern as old as existence itself, echoing through every workshop, studio, and garden where human hands bring new things into being. In this way, every act of creation becomes a kind of prayer—what Christians might call a participation in Divine co-creation, or what Hindus might recognize as karma yoga, the spiritual path of sacred action.

Earlier, I wrote about developing the true voice—how it takes time and requires deliberate, slow progress. It's not something you can rush. Earlier, I spoke about reincarnation, and about my belief that the soul's journey spans more than a single lifetime. As a child in Catholic school, I remember the nuns driving home the concept of mortal sin. Commit one, and you're done—your soul's fate is sealed. It was such a crushing notion that I'd think, *Why bother? If I'm already damned, what's the point of trying?* That kind of thinking can paralyze progress rather than inspire it. The Church's fear of complacency, of people taking their time to evolve, contrasts with what I've come to realize: we're *meant* to take our time. Thomas Merton, the great theologian, once said that sometimes God leaves souls blinded for God's good pleasure. Even God, it seems, enjoys watching life unfold at its own pace—like someone watching *Fawlty Towers*.

True growth, whether in art, spirituality, or life, requires patience. It's not about rushing to the finish line but about understanding that every step, no matter how small, contributes to the journey. Every moment shapes the voice we're meant to share with the world. When asked how long it took him to paint a picture, Picasso would say, "It took all my life." That's the truth of any great work, whether it's art, personal development, or spiritual evolution—it encompasses everything you've lived, experienced, and learned. There's no shortcut.

Besides, there's joy in the process, the gradual evolution of a soul. The path isn't always straight or clear. Even Merton said he doubted there was anyone who is absolutely free. At some point, we even have to become free of meditation and prayer. Monks, he explained, leave all their attachments to the world—cars, houses—only to form new attachments to prayer and meditation. Eventually, you have to give up those attachments, too.

This applies to everything, not just spiritual growth. As Buddha advised, we must walk the middle path, not veer into extremes, whether in effort or ambition. I've learned this firsthand. No matter how hard I've tried—living in monasteries, meditating, striving for enlightenment—you simply cannot force progress. You have to let it unfold naturally, like McCloskey's method of teaching singers: vocalizing gently for a year, building up slowly.

In Hinduism, they say that life itself is like a Divine screen, and when we die, we wake up, realizing this existence was like a dream. It takes countless lifetimes to evolve and truly grasp this concept. Thomas Merton once said that the best way to become a contemplative or mystic isn't necessarily through retreating from the world into monasteries or caves. It's about engaging with the world and learning from the messiness of life itself. Something that I have certainly tried to embrace.

Maybe in another lifetime, I'll have learned enough through successive lifetimes, but for now, the lesson is to stumble through, relying on intuition and experience. Looking back on my journey—from the violence of North End to the lightning strike, from business ventures to spiritual seeking—I see how each experience was necessary. Each struggle, each failure, each moment of clarity was part of understanding this deeper truth: that we're all participating in a Divine dance of creation, whether we realize it or not.

The Trinity isn't just a religious concept—it's a pattern that runs through everything. In business, in art, in love, in spiritual practice. When we align ourselves with this pattern, when we allow ourselves to be instruments of creation rather than forcing our will upon the world, that's when magic happens. That's when we become co-creators with the Divine.

And maybe that's the ultimate lesson: that Divinity isn't something distant and unreachable, but something we participate in every day through our thoughts, our actions, and our creations. Whether we're building a bench, hosting guests, or simply living our lives with awareness, we're all part of this eternal dance of thought, motion, and creation.

CHAPTER 18

Three Daughters

"Like King Lear, I learned that love doesn't always flow in straight lines"

One of my greatest acts of creation was of course my three beautiful daughters. (Of course, given my talk of the Trinity, there had to be three!) Unlike Lear, who demanded proclamations of love from his daughters before dividing his kingdom, I never sought such grand declarations. Instead, I learned to accept love in its many forms, even when it came wrapped in conflict and complexity.

Fatherhood has been a journey as complex as any spiritual quest. I have three daughters by three different women: Each relationship, each daughter, has brought her own lessons and revelations. Like Cordelia, Goneril, and Regan, each had her own way of expressing— or sometimes withholding—affection, though thankfully our story played out with far less tragedy than Shakespeare's tale.

Sarah was the first, born during my marriage to Donna.

She was so young when our relationship broke down, and our father-daughter relationship was strained by living apart. She ended up following the Grateful Dead, and I used to have to get in a car to drive down to Rhode Island and rescue her from some trouble or other. Unlike Lear, who banished his most honest daughter, I knew better than to let pride stand between me and my child, no matter how stark our differences. According to her teacher, she was quite the provocative child in school, and I was sad I didn't have more input into her path through life, but Donna fought me all the way. Even after we were forced to live miles apart, I still heard about Sarah from time-to-time, usually because she'd done some crazy thing or another.

It felt like we were born in conflicting incarnations, and we were never going to see eye-to-eye. That same violent temper that coursed through my mother runs in Sarah too. She had a volatile spirit, and could – and did – knock a guy out with one punch one time. (So, whatever happens in her life, at least I know that she can look after herself!)

Joanna came into my life in an entirely different way. After Donna, I was dating Annette, a French woman who was staying at Judge Aldrich's son's home. She had just left Paris after a difficult relationship and decided to come to the United States. She was politically intense, heavily involved in the May 1968 protests in Paris.[36] Her circle included people who fled to South America during that time. We started seeing each other, but her constant focus on politics was exhausting. She'd buy every newspaper and launch into tirades about injustice. I wasn't political then—it just wasn t my world. The relationship wasn't peaceful, and it wore me down.

What I didn't know was that Annette had decided, without telling me, to stop using birth control. The day I broke up with her—unable to handle the relentless intensity—was the day she found out she was pregnant. She chose not to tell me and returned to Paris to have the child. About a year or two later, I received a letter, with photographs. I didn't even need to read the letter—I looked at the photos and knew Joanna was my daughter. Annette wrote that she hoped Joanna would want to know her father someday and asked how I felt about it. Even though I'd initially been shocked to hear the news, I was absolutely elated, and wanted to have as much contact with my daughter as possible. I write to Anette saying, "My arms are wide open."

From then on, Joanna would spend summers with me. She grew up speaking fluent English, which helped, as the only French I knew was, "mon amour, je t'aime, ma chérie." Joanna was vibrant, spontaneous, and full of life—very French. We shared a similar sense of humor and would laugh endlessly. She was an absolute joy.

---

[36] Franco-American relations were particularly strained during the period of Annette's involvement in the May 1968 protests. The student uprising in Paris led to the largest general strike in French history, with 11 million workers participating.

Years later, Joanna got divorced and started dating a much younger man—half her age—a streetwise Arab-French guy from Paris. I told her it wouldn't work, and that the age gap would eventually become a problem, but she didn't listen. She even brought him to stay at my house, which created unbearable tension. That night, I collapsed at home. There was blood everywhere. It was chaos. My eyes rolled back in my head, and I fell, unconscious to the floor. I've been told that Joanna—thinking it was a stress response—said to Christy, "I think I killed my father." The ambulance came, and I remember feeling relief when they got me out of the house. But as they wheeled me out, I realized Joanna was in the ambulance with me, and I felt trapped all over again.

At the hospital, they couldn't find the source of the bleeding. I ended up in ICU surrounded by massive machines, unable to breathe. The thought of jumping off the hospital roof just to take a few deep breaths of fresh air crossed my mind. I felt like a prisoner. They wheeled me into what felt like the dungeons of Mass General—an underworld of eccentric but brilliant doctors working with enormous machines trying to figure out what was wrong. They eventually found the bleed and cauterized it, but not before I'd received 14 transfusions.

The effect of the transfusions was surreal. For a short time, I felt like I'd inherited traits from the donors. I suddenly craved cauliflower, which I'd hated my whole life. I couldn't wait to cook it with garlic and oil. I also found myself watching sports—something I'd never done. But after a couple of weeks, the cravings and habits disappeared. It was bizarre.

Joanna was deeply remorseful and asked for forgiveness, which I gave her. We've since healed emotionally, and our relationship is wonderful now. I've also built a great connection with my French grandchildren, who've visited and stayed here.

Then there's Ariel, my youngest, from my relationship with Susan. Susan and I met through a mutual connection at Boston University. She was a classical pianist (who knew Nadia Boulanger) in Paris. Susan had gone on to work in film after meeting a Harvard graduate who became a producer. She even starred in a Swedish movie, Christa, where she played the second lead. When the movie came to the U.S., it was rebranded with a more sensational title: *Swedish Fly Girls*. It was surreal sitting in the Exeter theater in Boston, watching Susan on the big screen while she sat next to me.

Ariel inherited Susan's artistic side but also shares a lot of my traits. She's brilliant and creative, with a spark that ties back to the women I've known and the life I've led. Each of my children connects to a different part of me, and though the journey hasn't always been smooth, I see pieces of myself in all of them.

My unbridled and devil-may-care creativity has surfaced in all of my children, particularly in my oldest daughter, Sarah. They each carry forward different aspects of my journey—the wildness, the creativity, the quest for understanding. Looking at them, I see how the Divine has a sense of humor, how it takes our traits and reshapes them in unexpected ways through our children.

When I think of King Lear and his daughters, I hope I've learned more from my experiences than he did from his. Where Lear's tragedy stemmed from his inability to accept love in its various forms, I've tried to embrace each daughter's unique way of showing affection. Each relationship, each daughter, has taught me something about love, about letting go, about accepting what is, rather than what we wish would be. They've been my greatest teachers in understanding that love, like spirituality, isn't something you can control or direct—it flows where it will, taking its own course, teaching its own lessons.

Unlike Lear's kingdom, which he tried to divide equally among his daughters, the inheritance I hope to pass on to my children isn't material wealth, but rather the richness of experience, the value of authenticity, and the understanding that love, in all its complicated forms, is worth preserving. In the end, perhaps that's where Lear and I differ most: while his story ended in tragedy born of pride and misunderstanding, I've learned to weather the storms of family life with patience and acceptance, finding beauty in the imperfect ways we show our love.

CHAPTER 19

Divine Comedy in the Hospital

"Even in ICU, there's always room for a punchline"

Towards the end of the process of writing this book, I took an ambulance to the emergency room at MGH Hospital. I tripped on a rug and went flying across the room. Luckily, I caught myself, because, as you'll have guessed, I obviously have wings!

At the hospital, my roommate was dying from cancer and heart failure. Despite the somber circumstances, I brought a lot of laughter to the ward. I heard a nurse say, "We can hear your roommate laughing all the way down on the floor below." I was telling jokes nonstop, and I think they discharged me after four days because I was just too happy for them to handle.

I often travel with a doctor friend, Arshad, who is legendary here in Cambridge. He's originally from Pakistan, a unique guy who has led a fascinating life. Sometimes we go to Chicago together, where his uncle, only a year older than him, worked as an ER doctor for decades. His uncle, Saleem, bought buildings in downtown Chicago, one of which he turned into a nightclub. He hired a top designer to transform the space, and now the lower floors are a live-music venue with food, drinks, and dancing, while the top two floors serve as his penthouse.

Once, I teased Saleem, "You haven't given up your medical license yet."

He said, "What are you talking about? Of course, I have."

I replied, "No, you haven't. People come here, drink, dance, laugh—you're still making them happy. It's just a different kind of medicine."

When one of Saleem's friends was dying of cancer, we went to visit him in the hospital. Bear in mind that Saleem is an internal medicine doctor, and Arshad, is an ER doctor. The man we visited was lying in the corner bed, barely able to open his eyes. You could see the sadness in him. A young doctor came by and introduced himself with a self-important air. "I'm Dr. So-and-So," he said, full of pomp.

I couldn't resist a joke. "Well, I'm Dr. Feelgood. Actually, my alias is Dr. Catizone. This is Dr. Ashad, and here's Dr. Saleem."

We all laughed, and then I took the floor. I told the dying man, "You know what you need? Some strippers to come in and cheer you up." His eyes lit up, and he smiled from ear to ear. For a moment, it brought him to life.

The head doctor, a Puerto Rican woman, came over to me, pressed her knees against mine, and said, "You're Italian, aren't you?" She could see it in me straightaway.

One time, my friend Hal, a gynecologist, invited me to an event at the State House. His sister-in-law—another doctor, and a good friend of mine—had passed away. It was a big gathering because Hal's son was in the legislature. There was this woman there, a fancy traveler with a sophisticated job, and she said, "I just flew in from Belgium." I replied, "I just came in from Hanover Street." That broke the ice. She realized how ridiculous it sounded to mention Belgium in that way. Little moments like that—breaking the ice—make everything flow.

To me, a real doctor doesn't flaunt the title. They say, "Hi, I'm Benny," with humility. That's true professionalism.

To me, it is a simple thing to administer some comedy to people in need. The jokes, the laughter, and the camaraderie all help brighten the spirits, even in those people meeting the end of their lives. Above all else, perhaps it is the camaraderie that matters most, an understanding that we're all destined to pass through our lives in double quick time, that whether we come round again or not, we're all just passing through.

It made me think: hospitals need comedians. People often tell me I should've been a stand-up comic. I say, "No, I'm a sit-down comic—I like to stay seated." A few times I've been a lying-down comic!

There's a story about Norman Cousins, the famous editor, who was dying of cancer. He found that every time he laughed—whether at a comedy show or a funny film—he felt better. He checked himself out of the hospital, rented a motel room, and surrounded himself with humor[37]. He laughed his way to recovery, curing himself... though he later died of a heart attack.

The doctors and nurses at MGH were extraordinary. I always tell my favorite nursing joke: A woman sees a nurse giving her father a sleeping pill and half a Viagra. She asks, "I understand the sleeping pill, but why half the Viagra?" The nurse replies, "That's so he doesn't roll out of bed." It always gets a laugh.

It's clear to me that healing isn't just about medicine, it's about caring for, and nourishing the spirit. Sometimes a laugh can do more than a pill. Like that time when I healed Sarah's stomach; I gained the power to heal her because I made the decision to stay in the marriage, and by sacrificing my own personal needs. I'm no saint, it was simply a mechanical process.

I see it now as part of the same Divine comedy that runs through everything. Even in the hospital, facing death or serious illness, there's room for joy, for connection, for transformation. The healing comes not just from the medicine but from the moments of genuine human connection, whether it's a shared laugh, a gentle touch, or a moment of understanding between patient and caregiver.

Maybe that's why I've always been drawn to doctors and healers as friends. They understand something essential about the human condition, that we're all vulnerable, all imperfect, all in need of both physical and spiritual healing. And sometimes the best medicine isn't in the IV drip, it's in the simple act of making someone smile when they thought they'd forgotten how.

---

[37] Norman Cousins (1915-1990), former editor of the Saturday Review, documented his experience using laughter as therapy in his 1979 book "Anatomy of an Illness." He developed a recovery program centered around positive emotions and laughter and reported that ten minutes of genuine belly laughter would give him two hours of pain-free sleep. His case was a landmark in the study of psychoneuroimmunology and the mind-body connection in healing.

The hospital is a strange place, like a monastery where the prayers are replaced by beeping machines. During my internal bleeding episode, when they couldn't find the source and I was hooked up to all those monitors in ICU, I had a lot of time to think about the relationship between body and spirit.

I remembered a psychiatrist once telling me that the moment of clarity comes after the decision is made. Before that, everything is chaos and panic, but once the choice is clear, there's peace. That resonated with me. I thought about Dirk, a friend of mine who had committed suicide in this life—and presumably in other lifetimes too—suggesting that if things got too tough for him, he would effectively check out.

In hindsight, I think I could've used humor in those in extremis moments. When Dirk told me he was leaving me some cigar paraphernalia, I could've asked, "What are you doing with your BMW?" Maybe that would've jolted him into reconsidering. But you always second-guess yourself after the fact.

The hospital showed me another side of healing too. A few years ago, I was at a Cambridge party filled with psychiatrists. A psychiatrist told me that when she was a young intern at Mass General Hospital, a guy arrived thinking he was a cow. Her Professor got down on all fours and started mooing like a cow! The guy immediately started to smile.

That's what I've come to see as emotional intelligence: the ability to feel, to connect, and to act intuitively in the moment. It's not about numbers or systems, it's about the human connection, the willingness to step into the unknown with grace. It's about falling in, not holding back. That's where the real magic happens.

I see the ambulance as my personal limousine now. It's bumpy, sure, but the drivers—usually women—always say, "It's the potholes." I tell them, "You don't need to go looking for the potholes!" They even put the siren on for me. At this point, they should have neon lights saying, "Catizone's on board."

I can have my cardiologist in stitches when I tell him, "What do you get when someone's part Jewish and part Italian? If they can't buy it wholesale, they steal it!" We always laugh a lot. Laughter is the best medicine, not because it cures anything and everything, but because it reminds us that we're more than just our ailments.

That's something I learned from those monastic days; the body isn't just a machine to be fixed, it's a vehicle for the soul. When I was in the Greek Orthodox monastery, the long hours of prayer would exhaust the body but somehow feed the spirit. It's the same in the hospital, sometimes healing comes not from fighting against what's happening to your body, but from finding a deeper peace with it.

Recently, I had another revelation about healing when I was bitten by a yellowjacket. I tried to gently put it outside with a paper towel, but it stung me through the towel. The pain was blinding; I saw stars. My first instinct was to kill it, but I stopped myself, thinking, *It's only doing what it knows to do.* I managed to get it outside, but that night I developed a fever, and my breathing became labored.

Curious, I looked up the mystical significance of a yellow jacket sting.[38] I read that in Native American traditions, wasp 'medicine' is often used to heighten the ability to navigate between different worlds (just as the wasps flit between air and earth). It is often regarded as purification or initiation experience. The intense pain and potential swelling represents a mini-ordeal that some traditions view as cleansing or transformative. That night, I had a dream where the yellowjacket appeared in human form. It was this vaudevillian character, glowing and dimming, full of himself. We talked—though I can't remember what we said—and it left me wondering about the meaning behind it all. Maybe it was just a dream, or maybe it was a sign to let go of the need for control, to trust the unknown.

I woke up thinking about the past and the future. About how I had kept elements of my parents alive after they had died, by absorbing aspects of their personalities into myself, and wondering if that was

---

[38] Of the interesting interpretations, I read that a yellowjacket sting is often seen as a wake-up call or message to pay attention to something you've been ignoring, their sharp sting serves as an abrupt alert. It has also been regarded as a purification or initiation experience, the intense pain and potential swelling represents a kind of mini-ordeal that some traditions view as cleansing or transformative.

my way of keeping them alive, preserving something of them in myself. And I was reminded of a vision of my own future that I'd had many years before: Walking out of my door in the North End, I suddenly saw a future life, clear as day hundreds of years in the future in which I was a kind of St. Francis figure. When I told my sister, she thought I was being an egomaniac, but it wasn't about grandeur, it was about considering how roles repeat themselves, how certain characters are best fit to replay certain scenes. I do believe we come back again and again, playing different roles, learning different lessons, and I woke up from that yellowjacket sting, wondering if all these times exist in parallel. Are we just a veil away from the 17th century century, or the 23rd century?

Like I mentioned earlier, I don't trust anyone who thinks I'm smart! But I'll accept 'unique'! In the North End, I acquired that reputation of being a cross between a monk and a wild guy, someone who didn't follow the rules. Even Airbnb tells guests I'm like 'the most interesting man in the world' from those beer commercials. But what makes me unique, I think, is that I have no guidelines. I'm wild in my thinking. I believe in leprechauns and elves and fairies, in things I can't see rather than what I can see. Mary understood this about me. She'd say, 'I'm always amazed at what you don't know, but I'm also amazed at what you do know.' I didn't know which ocean was which, but I could explain in two sentences what philosophers had argued about for centuries. She saw that my untrained brain, working without boundaries, could sometimes see things her Harvard-educated mind couldn't catch.

I've learned that even the bad experiences have their lessons. The hospital stays, the transfusions, the various close calls, they're all part of the same Divine comedy. Perhaps our bodies need their crises and transformations to help our souls grow. But I've also observed how healing isn't always about getting better, sometimes it's about understanding why you're sick in the first place. Every yellowjacket sting and every brush with mortality has struck me like another turn in that spiral of understanding. Each time I go around again, I arrive back at a parallel point with a slightly broader perspective. And maybe that's where the real healing happens, when we imbibe the wisdom we gain from each experience. Every crisis becomes a teacher, every recovery a kind of resurrection. Even the pain has its purpose, if we're willing to learn from it.

Those transfusions taught me something about identity too. When you're lying there receiving someone else's blood, you start to wonder: what makes us who we are? Is it our blood? Our memories? Our spirit? I had fourteen different people's blood flowing through my veins, and for a while, I was craving things I'd never wanted before. It was like hosting a committee meeting in my bloodstream, each donor getting a vote on what I should eat or watch on TV.

You see the same thing with heart transplant recipients sometimes. They start craving foods the donor liked, picking up habits they never had before. It makes you wonder about the connection between body and soul. Where does one end and the other begin? Maybe we're all just borrowing these bodies anyway, like rental cars for our souls. How much of what we think of as "us" is really ours?

Speaking of souls, there was this one night in ICU when I couldn't breathe properly. All these machines were beeping and whirring, and I had this overwhelming urge to get up to the roof, just to take one deep breath of fresh air. I was ready to drag all those machines with me if I had to. That's when I realized something else about healing, sometimes what your body needs and what your soul needs are two different things.

It reminds me of what Father Mark used to say at the monastery. As a monk and a medical doctor, he understood both sides, the physical and the spiritual. He'd tell me that sometimes the body's crisis is the soul's opportunity. Like when you have a fever - the discomfort is actually your body fighting off the infection. Sometimes you need to go through the fire to come out stronger.

I've noticed that doctors who understand this tend to be better healers. There was this old doctor at Mass General—he must have been in his eighties—who would come in at 3:00 am if he heard one of his patients was having trouble. He'd sit on the bed, hold their hand, and just talk. No prescriptions, no procedures, just presence. That's healing too.

But you know what really gets me? The way that everyone in the hospital—all the doctors, nurses, patients—all have their roles to play in the grand performance. The doctors with their important walks, the nurses with their efficient movements, the patients trying to be good patients, it feels like a big theater production. And then someone like me comes in and starts telling jokes, and suddenly the masks slip a little. We remember we're all just people trying to figure out life and death.

A joke, or a bit of gossip, or a big revelation all have the same effect, they can all break the spell. When you can get a dying man to laugh, even for a moment, you're reminding him that he's still alive. When you can make a stressed-out doctor smile, you're helping them heal too. We're all in it together.

I think back to those times in the monastery, when I'd try to sneak in meditation between prayers. The monks thought prayer was the only way to reach God, but I found Divine presence in breathing, in silence, in laughter. Healing isn't just fixing what's broken, it's remembering our wholeness. Whether it's through prayer or laughter, medicine or meditation, the goal is the same: to bring us back to ourselves, to remind us who we really are beneath all the pain and fear and confusion.

And sometimes, when you're lying in a hospital bed in the dead of night, watching the moon through the window and listening to the gentle beeping of machines, you get these moments of perfect clarity. You realize that all of it—the suffering and the joy, the sickness and the health—are all part of the same dance. The Divine comedy.

And maybe that's the biggest joke of all... In our moments of greatest weakness, we finally find our greatest strength. In our moments of deepest fear, we find our capacity for laughter. In our moments of most intense pain, we find our connection to something greater than ourselves. In our moments closest to death, we finally work out how to live.

The hospital, like life itself, is just another stage where we act out our parts, and if my role is to play the fool and bring some laughter to the show, I'll play my part with an eternal smile on my face.

CHAPTER 20

Something Worth Talking About

"God loves a good drama"

Life isn't about perfection, it's about the story, and as humans, our stories are full of mess and disorder. That's why Christ didn't choose perfect disciples, he picked fishermen, tax collectors, and misfits, people full of flaws, illiterates, nobodies. If it's an imperfect world, then how can the church or its people be perfect?

I've come to love the imperfect disciples. When I learned that Thomas Merton was a womanizer, I loved him even more. Because he was human. It's like why Peter, the imperfect disciple, was made head of the church, the church had to be imperfect so people could relate to it.

I have realised, and accepted—and even come to enjoy—the fact that the imperfections are what make our lives and our stories so compelling. It's clear that God loves a good drama, and every day, he proves himself to be quite the dramatist!

Looking back at my own story—from the violence of North End to the lightning strike, from business ventures to spiritual seeking—I see how each experience was not only necessary, but worthwhile. Each struggle, each failure, each moment of clarity was part of understanding this deeper truth: that we're all just playing at life, dancing to different tunes until we figure out our own.

My life has played out in three acts. Act One was all violence and early seeking, stumbling through the streets of North End while carrying those early meditative experiences from my attic room. I was living two lives even then: the tough kid who could handle himself in a fight, and the young seeker watching the sunlight move across his floor.

Act Two began with that lightning strike in St. Stephen's. I was an angry young man from the streets, and God chose to use nature's own fireworks to facilitate my transformation. It wasn't subtle, but then again, neither was I. That led to my testing period as I tried to understand what had happened to me, learning to channel this new energy through helping others, even the wiseguys who came in search of some understanding.

Act Three has been about integration, bringing together all these seemingly contradictory parts of myself. The street kid who could discuss philosophy, the businessman who understood Eastern mysticism, the artist who could talk to MIT professors about Aristotle. Even now, hosting people from around the world in our Airbnb, I'm still integrating, still performing, still finding new ways to share what I've learned.

Through all of this, I kept seeing the same pattern emerge: thought, motion, creation. It's how I came to understand the Trinity as something more than an abstract theological concept, and understood it instead as a living process that runs through everything. I saw it in my art. When I would fast and meditate, positioning myself like an antenna to receive the energy or consciousness that wanted to come through, that was thought. The physical work with materials—copper, brass, steel, silver, glass, fire—that was motion. The finished piece that seemed to have its own energy field, that was creation.

Even in business, with Body Roc, the pattern was there. The initial idea of sticking a diamond to my shoulder was thought. All those months in libraries researching adhesives, flying to London, setting up manufacturing—that was motion. The final product, even though it didn't last, was creation.

But here's where the comedy comes into the drama; the pattern doesn't always play out the way you expect. Sometimes the creation doesn't yield what you thought you were creating at all. Take my time in Oregon. I thought I was building a cabin for my family, but what I was really creating was a deeper understanding of myself. The three streams of water I channeled into one became my own physical demonstration of the Trinity, teaching me about unity and flow in a way no book or teacher could have.

The same thing happened with relationships. Each one was like its own Divine comedy, complete with dramatic entrances, plot twists, and unexpected revelations. Verdi would have loved writing about how I stole Donna from a wiseguy, was taken out into the woods at night and menaced by El Cid and his knives, then ended up getting married in a funeral parlor. I like to think God had a good laugh at seeing how it all played out.

Every relationship taught me something different about Divine love, usually in ways I never expected. Like when I met Andrea after my year of celibacy. Abandoning celibacy for worldly pleasure, and then feeling God's absolution. The irony was of course that having granted me love, God took it away again. But there were lessons to be learned in first accepting love and then in letting it go.

I had to learn about peace in the most violent way possible; when that lightning struck St Stephens it felt as if the world was being torn asunder! Even my time in the monasteries played into the Divine sense of humor, as I snuck meditation sessions between prayer sessions. How ridiculous must I have seemed, changing my posture whenever I heard footsteps so the monks wouldn't catch me doing anything 'off brand'. I was starring in my own spiritual sitcom, dancing to the tune of religious fusion, while the monks kept time to a different drum. I think I've given God plenty to laugh about.

In my meditative sate, I felt as if I was actually talking with God, and I think He liked that. (Perhaps, God gets lonely sometimes. Perhaps that's why he created us in the first place.) And, just like any artist, he enjoys watching his creation unfold in unexpected ways. That's what I learned from all my relationships, and all my spiritual experiments; the Divine isn't some stern taskmaster demanding perfection, he's more of a playwright who loves improv and can't resist throwing new characters and opportunities into our lives just to see what we'll do with them.

I reflect on all of these things now, when I play host to people from around the world. The street kid who once dodged police and slashed tires is now entertaining guests with stories about those very same streets. I can't help but admire the perfect symmetry at work here.

Of course, North End has changed as I have. The streets and

communities are very different than they were in the nineteen fifties and sixties.[39] In the 50s, there were 60,000 Italians packed into one square mile - a pressure cooker of culture, tradition and intrigue. Hanover Street was our Broadway, our forum, our community center all rolled into one. You couldn't walk ten feet without someone pulling you into their doorway for an espresso or stopping you to share the latest gossip.

But the neighborhood transformed. The old Italians started dying off or moving out to the suburbs. Their children chose different lives. The yuppies moved in, complaining about the church bells that had rung for generations. The rents skyrocketed. Shops that had been in families for decades closed or got converted into boutiques.

Some changes were inevitable. The violence that defined our era faded. You don't see kids getting their PhD in tire slashing anymore. The mafia's grip loosened. Even the restaurants changed, now they cater more to tourists than to locals. But certain things endure: the smell of gravy cooking on Sundays, old men playing cards in the cafes, the way arguments still sound like scenes from opera performances.

The North End today is like a sanitized version of what it used to be. Still beautiful in its way, but the rawness that made it what it was has been polished away. I still think that something essential remains. You can still sense it in the narrow streets and ancient buildings, in the way people still gather for the feasts and processions, in how neighbors still know each other's business, there's an echo of what it was. And maybe that's how it should be. Nothing stays the same forever. The neighborhood, like me, had to transform to survive.

I have adapted too. Content with what I have learned about life, and about my path through many lives. I'm still the seeker of life's secrets, and still the raconteur. My life as an Airbnb host gives me the perfect excuse to go on performing. Every new guest gets to be a part of this story, just as I intersect with theirs, and I like to think that we each

---

[39] The transformation of Boston's North End continues: by 2020, only 30% of residents claimed Italian ancestry, compared to 90% in 1950. However, the neighborhood retains the highest concentration of Italian restaurants in New England.

leave the other, richer for the experience of our chance meeting.[40] Sometimes these impromptu performances yield unexpected miracles. Like when that man thanked me for making his wife smile again after their son had been murdered in San Francisco. Transformation isn't always about dramatic change; these small moments of connection, of shared humanity, they may not be the dramatic transformations of lightning strikes, but they're just as transformative in their own way.

After all of my spiritual seeking, after all my experiments with monasticism and meditation, I've ended up exactly where I started: telling stories in North End. But now I understand something I didn't before: that the Divine reveals itself not just in burning bushes and lightning strikes, but in the simple act of making someone laugh, of sharing a story, of creating a moment of connection. That's what all those years of studying the Trinity have taught me, that we're all co-creators in this Divine comedy. Every thought we have, every move we make, everything we create becomes part of the larger performance. Whether we're building a meditation bench or telling a joke to strangers, we're participating in the same creative force that moves through everything.

Looking back now, I can see that every part of my journey was necessary, even the parts that seemed like cosmic jokes at the time. That violent kid in North End, the young seeker, the street fighter turned spiritual advisor, the businessman, the artist, the host— they're all just different roles that I've played. Through all the faces I've worn, and the experiences I've had, I've seen that being spiritual isn't about escaping the world - it's about finding your way through it. When Rasputin was asked whether the voice of God came from inside or outside himself, he answered, 'There's no difference.' That's Divine madness, understanding that all these divisions we make are part of the illusion. The moon is right here. There's no separation between the sacred and the ordinary, between inside and outside. It's all one

---

[40] The tradition of Italian-American storytelling has roots in the cantastorie (story-singers) of southern Italy. These performers would combine personal narrative with social commentary, much like the modern practice of "holding court" in Italian-American communities.

continuous dance.

My grandfather from Naples would say, "Pietro, you've got to talk about something." Well, this has been my something: a story about violence and peace, about performance and authenticity, about finding grace in the space between Christianity and Eastern spirituality. About learning that the Divine has a sense of humor, and that sometimes the most spiritual path is the one that makes you laugh.

In the end, maybe that's what this journey has really been about— learning to dance with the Divine, to play my part in the cosmic comedy while staying true to my own voice. Whether I'm entertaining guests, crafting art, or just living my daily life, I'm still performing, still creating, still participating in this grand improvisation. I'm part of a long tradition of Italian storytellers stretching back many years.

People often say, "I can't believe you've never been to Italy." At a dinner party once, surrounded by academics with houses in Normandy and Paris, they couldn't believe that, apart from England, I'd never been to Europe. My friend Vincent Rochento, who we called "Little Mozart" because he was a violin genius, said, "Why does Peter need to go to Italy? Peter's got sunny Italy inside him." That's how I've always felt—like wherever I go, I carry the essence of the place within me. Just as I carry all of my experiences from this life—and those that I believe have come before.

A psychic once told me I'd been imprisoned in a dungeon in England centuries ago. He described me as well-dressed, someone of royal blood or means, who had their land and money taken by the establishment. Apparently, I was really pissed off about that! Another psychic said I had been trying to reform the system legally but had been targeted. True or not, I do know that when I was in London, I felt an uneasiness, as though I'd lived through something there. At the same time, it felt like home.

To me, the concept of reincarnation fits so beautifully into the puzzle of existence. Life, like philosophy, is a toolbox, and we take on those things that help us from one life to the next. And here I am now, with Buddhist pliers, Hindu screwdriver, and Christian hammer, all helping me to shape my understanding and find equilibrium as God watches on.

These days, I watch very little news. Technology is wonderful, but it brings all the bad stuff right to our doorstep. Instead, I try to become more and more absorbed in the consciousness of God. The truth is that life has to be difficult—it's our spiritual gym—but you have to keep your calm at the center of it all, doing the things that feel authentic to you. Which is why I'm still here, still telling stories, still trying to make sense of it all. That feels right to me. That feels as close to following my dharma as I'm going to get.

In this Divine comedy, I believe there is no final curtain, no last act. There's just this ongoing dance of thought, motion, and creation. And as long as I'm breathing—in this life or the next—I'll keep dancing, keep performing, keep creating—because that's what I'm here for. That's the only way I know how to participate in the Divine.

As my 103-year-old grandfather from Naples would say, "That's something worth talking about."

Well readers, this has been my something - this long, strange journey from violence to peace, from the streets to the spirit, from confusion to clarity and back again. And somehow, it all makes perfect sense, even when it makes no sense at all.

That's the real miracle - not the lightning strike, but what comes after. The slow understanding that every moment is a chance for transformation, every story a kind of prayer, every connection a glimpse of the Divine. Even now, especially now, when a room full of strangers becomes friends, the Trinity reveals itself: in thought, in motion, in creation.

And if God is watching - and I'm sure He is - I hope He's been royally entertained. After all, he may have written a script outline, but I've been improvising like mad to fill in the interesting bits. Even now, I often joke and say that God and I used to double date. He'd always get a couple of angels for us to take out to dinner, and of course, I always made him look good. (I was a good wingman!) But beneath the joke is something true: that kind of intimacy with the Divine is possible.

APPENDIX 1

Doing the Deal (Vinnie's Story)

He was a mystery. If you asked fifty people who knew him (or knew of him) who he was, you would get fifty different descriptions. But all agreed he was untouchable.

When he was growing up in the North End of Boston in the 1940s and 1950s, he was Vinnie; at Boston Latin he was Vin, or just plain "Di Gangi". When guiding the careers of singing legend, Frankie Laine, and boxing legend, Roberto "Manos de Piedra" Duran, he was Vince. When living in Rome and Sicily in the 1990s he was Vincenzo, the name that followed him as Publisher of Boston's *North End Magazine* and stuck all through his adult life.

His reputation for integrity always followed him. He was a Man of Honor in the tradition of La Famiglia Di Gangi of Nociazzi, Sicily.

The early 1980s were not a good time for the Boston branch of La Cosa Nostra. Gennaro Angiulo and his brothers were in federal jails serving long sentences. No matter what one thinks of Gerry Angiulo and his leadership qualities, he was a moneymaker and did his time in prison like a man. However, when he went to federal prison, Angiulo took his money off the street... a disaster for the leadership that followed him, but an opportunity for Vincenzo Di Gangi.

One of the two new leaders (in Boston) was Dominic F. Isabella of the notorious Isabella family of Prato La Serra Italy, and New York City. Isabella's grandfather served under Di Gangi's grandfather, Calogero Di Gangi, in the early 1900s when Calogero Di Gangi was the "Boss" in Boston, not unlike Joe "The Boss" Masseria in New York City. This is what established the strong bond between the families that continued with Dominic and Vincenzo. And why Isabella told the 45-year-old Di Gangi of the predicament of the new leadership seven "made" members, of whom, one was already in jail.

Vinnie immediately offered to get the needed funds from his uncle "Gusty Pete's" 1930s partner, "Doc" Sagansky. Not possible because they had already gotten $250,000 and divided it giving $10,000 to the imprisoned member and $40,000 each to the other six. That was peanuts: Vinnie offered to secure five million from allies of the Di

Gangi family in Sicily. Dominic okayed this move, so Vinnie, with his wife, Heloisa, took off to the island.

A Baron friend of the Di Gangi's had arranged a meeting for the last day of his stay in Palermo. Of course, the lenders would be assembled to hear Vinnie's proposal. Vinnie and his wife arrived promptly at the antique business of the Baron, which was conveniently located one block away from their hotel. This proximity was set up because Vinnie had to catch a 6:00 AM flight to Rome for a connection to Boston.

On the second floor of an old Palermo building, which the Baron probably owned, Vinnie and Heloisa were welcomed into the dark suite with books and old maps laying everywhere. This was not the meeting place, obviously. Vinnie wanted to get in bed by 8:00 PM but the Baron seemed in no rush. At 7:00 PM the Baron escorted Heloisa into another room where the TV was showing Frank Sinatra in concert in Milan.

Vinnie's only hope at this stage was that the lenders would now appear, as his wife was wisely tucked away with Sinatra. All hopes were dashed when the Baron said they were going out for a dinner of Pasta Fagioli; Vinnie had always thought that was for poor people.

The Baron directed Vinnie to a modern edifice in Palermo, but in the same old section. They were not going to eat in a Ristorante, but in the gigantic, modern apartment of a Contessa.

Upon arrival, they were greeted by a beautiful blonde lady with her hair pulled back in a tight knot, and by her boyfriend, who was a Director of Banco di Roma. They were escorted into a large room, with a small table and two sofas-for-two between them in a corner. Then they were asked to sit for drinks and trays of delicate Sicilian food bits.

The four engaged in a lovely conversation for about 10 or 15 minutes, and then had to greet the second couple to arrive, who were brought over to sit on the sofa previously occupied by the 50-ish blonde Contessa. After another fifteen minutes, another couple was brought in to sit with Vinnie and Heloisa, who was a stunner in her own right... a gorgeous Northern Italian via Rio de Janeiro.

This protocol continued for around an hour when suddenly, white-jacketed waiters appeared to serve room-temperature Pasta e Fagiolo. Vinnie had never eaten this dish which he had only seen served hot. Here, it was served correctly, and it was fantastic. Vinnie had a second dish. Then came the filet mignon, which was so soft it fell apart.

After three hours, the Sicilians had had their meeting. Ten million dollars would be placed under Vinnie's supervision.

No board room, with a long, wooden conference table, no meeting brought to order, no notepads on the table... just room temperature Pasta e Fagioli.

Dominic Isabella was elated and the deal was on the launching pad until all seven "made" men were told all their assets had to be put up as collateral. Plus, they realized that Vinnie would be the real "Boss". Everything came to a halt and Vinnie never did business with any of the six, as Dominic died soon after.

The other six "made" men were soon in federal prisons for a long time.

The reputation of La Famiglia Di Gangi of Nociazzi made the deal... the Sicilians with their multiple Pasta e Fagiozi interviews wanted to know only if they would be comfortable working with Vinnie and Heloisa.

Vinnie never even made a proposal.

APPENDIX 2

The Omni Bench

The Original/traditional Japanese Seiza Meditation Bench had a set angle that a Buddhist monk thought of centuries ago which limited comfort and freedom. I re-designed the bench with a distinctive rounded leg base that allows for individual adjustment and spinal alignment allowing the meditator to sit comfortably for long periods of time whether in meditation or in simple relaxation. This unique design of the Omni meditation bench is especially helpful for people with back problems. The second requirement was to make the legs fold easily for portability and storage. So I designed and manufactured a spring cam system hinge that, when the legs were in either an opened or closed position, they would lock in position stabilizing the Omni Meditation Bench when being used in an opened position or closed for portability and storage.

Technically, I originally achieved this by modifying the knuckle structure of the hinges and also placing a spring in a linear position within the knuckle, so whether your opening or closing the bench legs when hitting the 30° linear angle from either the opened or closed position, the cam would activate the directional force of the spring from linear to horizontal.

Custom Benches

I have spoken with and made custom Benches for Phil Jackson, who was the head coach of the Los Angeles Lakers, considered one of the greatest coaches in NBA history, nicknamed "the Zen Master", and a former NBA player. As a coach, Jackson holds the NBA record for most championships with 11, and was named NBA Coach of the Year in 1996. Jackson's coaching style was unorthodox, drawing on Eastern philosophy and Native American mysticism. He's known for his holistic approach to mentoring and motivating players, and his leadership style has influenced many coaches and players.

I made custom light weight Omni benches for people traveling the Himalayas studying with Tibetan masters.

I would even get phone calls from the Middle East' one man told me I was famous in the Middle East because all the Sufi masters were using the Omni Meditation Benches for their students

Testimonials from my Omni Meditation Bench Customers

"The Omni Meditation Bench is by far the best sitting bench on the market."
—Pacific Spirit

"Your bench has helped my lower back problems immeasurably. I can now meditate without pain."
—D.P., Berkeley, California

"I have lower back pain which interferes with my meditation. A friend with similar problems told me with great excitement and enthusiasm what the Omni Bench had done for him. He let me borrow his bench. It was wonderful. Please send me an Omni Bench as soon as possible."
—S.B., Concord, California

"The bench has arrived. Thanks for the prompt service. Your product is just right for me as I have a spinal disorder which limits my meditation. Using the bench has about doubled the time in which I can sit and be pain free."
—Dr. C.B., Victoria, Australia

"Just a wonderful bench, feels just right for my back. I can understand why you have so many testimonials."
—C.S., El Cerrito, California

"Dear Mr. Catizone, I would like to thank you very much for the Omni Bench. It helps my back, I appreciate it. Now I am able to sit in meditation more often, thanks to you. Thank you very much."
—S.W., Gardner Prison, Gardner, Massachusetts

"A friend let me borrow his Omni Bench and it was fabulous. Please send me a large Omni Bench as soon as possible. Hi Peter — I just wanted to say thank you for such a wonderful bench. It arrived in only 3 days. I've been using it since, and it is amazing — no more screaming back! It will also be useful in playing with my 3 year old niece, as we spend a lot of time coloring on the floor. Thanks again."
—J.K., Toronto, Ontario, Canada

"Dear Peter, The kneeling bench you sent me last September is wonderful. I use it for drawing as well as meditation. It's amazingly comfortable for my back. It's the best portable seat by far that I've ever tried. Eventually I want to get that table you make to go with the bench. Many thanks for designing and making such a functional beautiful object."
—C.B., New York, New York

"Dear Peter, Upon first seeing my Omni, I immediately was impressed by the great karma ingrained not only by the tree which gave her up but by the artist who had created her as well. Since receiving her she has traveled 7 states with me and has served me well. I continue to be impressed by her beauty and utility. Zazen is no longer physically impossible for me with my arthritic knees and back. Thank you for your craftsmanship."
—J.B.F., Clinton, Missouri

"Dear Peter: Thank you for the prompt delivery of my Omni Bench. It is a wonderful piece of furniture, sturdily constructed, compact, and very light. It will be very easy to transport place to place. As soon as it arrived I just had to try it out. Now my meditation will not be plagued by stiff knees and ankles. It keeps my back nicely balanced. It is very comfortable to use. I will certainly recommend the Omni Bench to all inquirers with (and without) stiff joints."
—B.O., Toronto, Ontario, Canada

"Greetings! My Omni bench had arrived a few days prior to Christmas, but I restrained myself and refused to open it till Christmas morning. Not versed in all the various means of achieving enlightenment, while I was seated upon the Omni bench it was as near to enlightenment that I had as of yet achieved. Great bench and it really takes the pressure away from one's legs, thereby alleviating discomfort, and enabling one to maintain a straight back. Perfect for Zen meditation!!! Thanks!

If I am ever able to start my own Zen Judo school these benches will be used by the practitioners to better their meditation skills and in the process be granted the means to enlightenment."
—M.M., Akron, Ohio

"Dear Peter, A couple of weeks ago, I had an opportunity to try out my new Omni bench in an extended sitting situation. I was recording an intensive in Berkeley, with my teacher Pema Chodron. The place was jammed to the rafters. For two days, I was shoehorned behind a tiny sound table with the PA guy. One of his speaker stands was a couple of inches in front of my nose. He was sitting on a gomden, as were most of the people there. In this intensely claustrophobic situation, I discovered an unexpected benefit of my bench: it allowed me to occupy significantly less floor space than would have been the case with a cushion. I was deeply grateful to avoid the otherwise inevitable butting up of knees with my neighbor.

Other than that, my experience with the Omni has been that my back is a lot straighter, with less effort; and after an initial breaking-in period, I soon transcended the unfamiliarity of an uncushioned surface and minor foot discomfort. All in all, I much prefer the Omni to my gomden — in fact, I've started taking it with me to sitting events where I would otherwise have used the resident gomdens. It's so compact and light, I don't think twice about tucking it under my arm for the ride.

Once again, thank you for being so responsive, easy to work with, and generous. I expect my Omni bench to take me through many, many hours of posturally advanced practice."
—J.W., Boulder, Colorado

"Dear Peter, My bench arrived last Friday, and I wanted to contact you as soon as possible to say how delighted I am with it. Not only is it beautifully crafted and a joy to look at, but functionally it is soooooooo comfortable. Goodbye sciatica!! Sincere thanks and best wishes."
—S.T., Christ Church, Barbados

"Thank you for your help and wonderful meditation bench. On long retreats, its design allows minor adjustments of the angle of the spine which makes all the difference! We just finished our January retreat and your benches were the talk of the retreat, as they eased the pain of long meditation sessions."
—T.A., Esoteric Buddhist Society, Hawaii

"Peter, The bench has arrived and is proving to be well worth the wait. The custom fit is perfect and the bench is truly adding comfort to my

sitting practice. Thanks so much for making such a beautiful meditation bench for me."
—M.R., Carteret, New Jersey

"I am very impressed and happy with my Omni Bench, and look forward to receiving my Omni Desk. Your workmanship is exceptional and your obvious dedication to your craft enriches all who experience your products."
—K.J., Ph.D., Chicago, Illinois

"The design and workmanship is excellent. You have such a beautiful product."
—S.C., Freestone, California

"The Omni Bench has an elegant simplicity that reminds me of Shaker pieces."
—P.M., Philadelphia, Pennsylvania

"Thank you for such careful and fine workmanship and the care you have taken with this order."
—R.U., Lancashire, England

"The Omni Bench is excellent."
—P.P., Alberta, Canada

"I want to tell you how much I enjoy and appreciate this beautiful meditation bench. It's just a lovely piece."
—G.P., Kingston, Rhode Island

"It's beautiful. I love the hinges."
—L.F., Weston, Massachusetts

"I'm calling to tell you I really enjoy The Omni Bench. It's beautiful and your workmanship is excellent on the bench."
—B.D., Tracy, California

"It is beautifully done."
—B.F., Solana Beach, California

"I want to purchase an Omni Bench. Two of my friends ordered them and they think that they are just wonderful."
—K.A., Ponte Vedra, Florida

"Just got home from work. The bench was waiting for me at the

doorstep. I opened it up and sat on it for thirty seconds and it is so beautiful and so comfortable and I am so happy that I just had to call you right this minute and say thank you for creating such a beautiful piece of art. It's just absolutely gorgeous to look at. I love the grain that's in the seat — it's very unique — and I know it's going to help my meditation immeasurably because it just feels wonderful to sit on and I just wanted to thank you."
—Dr. B.F., Tampa, Florida

"I'm ordering an Omni Desk. I am anxious for its arrival based on the fine craftsmanship of the two benches of yours which I already have. Thank you for making such fine items. I will cherish them for the balance of this lifetime."
—J.C., Marysville, Ohio

"Thanks for the great benches!"
—T.P., Santa Rosa, California

"I see by your WWW address that you must be a sculptor. I would suspect that this explains the quality of your design which is apparent even in the pictures you sent."
—B.P., Denver, Colorado

"Thank you for your efficient service. I tried the bench today and it's wonderful."
—C.A., Montreal, Canada

"I just received the bench and it looks terrific. I will let my friends know."
—J.F., Los Angeles, California

"Dear Peter, I wanted to let you know how well your Omni Bench worked for me at my first retreat at Cloud Mountain Retreat Center (near Mt. Saint Helens). It is a very comfortable style of sitting for me in general, especially for meditation, as well as being a beautiful piece of furniture. Thank you."
—S.F., Poulsbo, Washington

"By the way the workmanship in the bench is just perfect."
—W.H., Northern California

"The bench came, it is to die for, bless you, it is wonderful."

—M.G., Kentfield, California

"I am really pleased with the bench."
—L.S., Cincinnati, Ohio

"A zafu user since 1950, I threw away my cushion after trying your bench."
—Abbot R.L., Zen Buddhist monastery, Chicago, Illinois

"I received your Omni Bench and I love it. I love that color oak, too. Again, I love the bench. It's beautiful and I'd like to order a desk to go with it."
—T.P., Portland, Oregon

"Thank you in advance. Again, I love my Omni Bench and I'm sure the Omni Desk and The Altar will be wonderful additions."
—C.R.S., Rocky River, Ohio

"Received my sitting bench today... many thanks for your kindness. It feels wonderful after years on the 'shifting buckwheats'... I expect that it will last through my lifetime. I will be sure that my son receives it when I can no longer have need for it, assuring its human contact beyond our lifetimes... My love and appreciation."
—B.F., Palos Verdes Estates, California

"The bench is great, very comfortable and a beautiful design."
—S.P., Salvador, Brazil

"Your pieces are lovely and very functional."
—N.K., Tucson, Arizona

"The wood you use — and your workmanship — is so beautiful."
—J.A., Napa, California

"Dear Peter: The bench arrived on Friday and is every bit as beautiful as I had imagined it would be! I took it to the zendo yesterday and proudly showed it off to my teachers. Using this bench, I was not reluctant to take a place closer to the front of the room, so that my hearing aids were more efficient in allowing me to hear the dharma talk. I used it on the straw mat, so that it would not slide on the wooden floor. The height proved to be exactly right. I am very, very pleased with it and thank you so much for figuring out how to construct it for my needs. Being in correspondence with you has been

a pleasure — using your craftsmanship will be a lifelong one."
—J.A., Napa, California

"I have just received the Omni Bench and it's all that I had hoped it would be."
—W.H., Ossining, New York

"Peter: You can add the names of K.T. and L.K. to those who find your Omni meditation benches the essence of elegant simplicity; not to mention great zazen facilitators."
—K.T.- L.K. St. James, New York

"Peter: Thanks for your craftsmanship."
—C-K.H., Tenafly, New Jersey

"Peter: The bench has arrived and it is exactly what I wanted. I think your desk and altar are really beautiful."
—M.B., Pacific Palisades, California

"Peter: Many thanks for supplying us with such a beautiful object to help us in those long sits!"
—K.L., Getreidegasse, Salzburg

"Peter: Thank you for a wonderful bench and prompt service."
—M.G. Winnipeg, Manitoba, Canada

"Peter: Bench is wonderful! Looking forward to the desk — rush it along!"
—T.B., Greenbelt, Maryland

"Peter: The Lord give you Peace. I just wanted to thank you for your prompt deliverance of the Omni Bench. I find it an excellent piece of work that allows me to maintain a more reverent stance before the Lord in prayer."
—E.J., Franciscan Friars of St. Bonaventure Friary, Brighton, Massachusetts

"Peter: Yesterday afternoon, much to our delight, the shrine table [Altar] was delivered. What a beautiful, beautiful shrine table. We are just thrilled with it. I cannot find the words to describe its beauty and that's an understatement. Our friends arrived as we were unpacking it and they were just as awestruck by its beauty and power. I cannot thank you enough."

—Professor F.J., Kalamazoo, Michigan

"The Altar is stunning. What an excellent craftsman you are, and the wood is beautiful."
—Dr. P.C., Nashville, Tennessee

"Thanks so much for the opportunity to choose the bench that most invariably met my comfort needs. Your workmanship is outstanding and the design aesthetically beautiful.

I am sure I'll be receiving inquiries into the source and I will enthusiastically refer them to you without reservation. Thanks again for your kindness and flexibility in accommodating my interest."
—S.K., San Francisco, California

"Dear Peter, Thanks for the great benches."
—T.R., Santa Rosa, California

"Dear Peter, What a wonderful product you are supplying."
—V.L., Gainesville, Florida

"Greetings Peter. I am so enjoying my bench — thank you. I would now like to order a desk and another bench for a friend. Thank you again for your fine work."
—J.H., San Francisco, California

"I just wanted to let you know that the altar arrived today and it is most gorgeous. It is extraordinary. You have outdone yourself and I love it. I wouldn't change a thing about it. Your aesthetic calls are wonderful and your galactic swirl is just great. Thanks so much. I appreciate all your good efforts."
—G.H., Inverness, California

"I received my bench today, and it's beautiful; had just returned from dropping my check in the mail to you, and it appeared like magic. Thanks again."
—D.A.W., New York, New York

"Dear Peter, The parcel arrived safely. Thank you so much for your efforts. The meditation bench is perfect in its elegant simplicity and functionality. I love it. You do good work. I'll contact you again regarding a further order (my wife covets your work.) Thanks again. All the best."

—Dr. E.F.C., Visiting Fellow, Chung-Ang University, Seoul, South Korea

"Dear Peter, THE BENCH ARRIVED TODAY! It could have a real positive effect on my sitting practice. Thanks for your prompt attention to this order and for a great product."
—P.R., Wantagh, New York

"Peter, I am enjoying the bench! It's really great. I feel like I'm in a yoga pose while meditating, only I'm totally comfortable."
—K.E. McD., Albany, California

"Hello Peter, I just got my meditation bench and couldn't wait to try it out! It is beautiful, and it is comfortable. I've been sitting full lotus for years, but now I have converted. I don't want to do anything to ruin the aesthetics of this beautiful piece of art."
—J.G., Narberth, Pennsylvania

"Dear Peter, I got the desk and bench today — they are wonderful. Thanks."
—S.N.D., Queensbury, New York

"Hello, I got to try one of your benches this weekend — I loved it. I think I want to order a bench along with a desk. Thanks."
—S.N.D., Queensbury, New York

"Thanks for the bench. It arrived two days ago and the wood is beautiful. Thanks."
—D.T., San Mateo, California

"Dear Peter; I have been meaning to write, but got busy with other things — the usual excuse of today. I received the large Figured Birch Omni Chair and I love it — the comfort, quality and care that you put into it are beautiful. Thank you again. There is a remote chance that I will be in New England in August for a meeting in Plymouth, NH. and after 10 years away from NE I will have to see Boston and Cambridge again and hope to stop in to thank you personally."
—Professor J.W.A., Claremont, California

"I just wanted to let you know that I received the benches today and they are stunning! I now understand what you meant when you talked about the beauty of the medium-sized beech bench. I have to admit that I hope my boyfriend prefers the large bench, because I

selfishly want the medium one for myself! If the large bench is too tall for his comfort, though, I'll have to give him the medium — exchange the large one for another medium for myself. Sigh. Thank you again, very much!"
—K.C.

"Dear Peter — My boyfriend and I used the benches for the first time this morning, and they work perfectly for him. So I get to keep the medium bench I love so much. And he was thrilled with the gift. Thank you again."
—K.C.

"My boyfriend and I have been using the meditation benches every day, and we love them! They are incredibly comfortable!"
—K.A.C., Oakland, California

"My friend told me you have the best bench on the market and so I would like to order one."
—R.D., Richmond, Virginia

"Peter, When I opened the box at first and saw the legs lying flat, my first thought was — how did he do that? Then I saw. How ingenious! In the parlance of the day — way cool!! I am so pleased to have the bench. The care and attention you gave to its creative design and precise construction are imminently apparent. I feel certain it will serve me well for many years to come. Thank you for accommodating my request in the height of the bench. My knees thank you as well! You can be sure that I will pass your name along with the highest of recommendations to anyone who wonders where I got such a finely considered object."
—J.B., Tampa, Florida

"Peter: I got it today, it looks great! Thanks."
—P. McC., San Diego, California

"Dear Peter, Just wanted to let you know I received the Omni bench you sent me today. I am delighted that I received it in time to go to my retreat. It's a beautiful bench and I think it will facilitate a much more comfortable sitting for me. Thanks once again!"
—C.S., Eugene, Oregon

"Received bench thanks. Looks great."

—S.E., Vancouver Island, BC, Canada

"Dear Mr. Catizone, I would like you to know that I have been a very happy user of one of your Omni benches that I purchased at a retail outlet in Seattle."
—Rev. E.N., Portland, Oregon

"Greetings! I have received a beautiful Omni Bench for Valentine's Day."
—L.H., Oakland, California

"Dear Peter Catizone, I would like to order an Omni Bench from you. It sounds perfect."
—J.M.P., Bellingham, Washington

"I'm happy to say your Omni Bench arrived safely today — a new sitting experience! Thanks for the prompt service."
—C.C., Eichenau, Germany

"Dear Peter, It was such a joy to speak with you over the phone. I wanted to thank you for your dedication to your work and your immediate friendship. I am looking forward to using your bench and telling others about it. I will be sure to contact you after I receive the benches.

I got the Omni Bench or both of them today, and they are fabulous, I really love it. I would like to talk to you more about expressing my adulation, it's really an amazing item, and I know, I have been doing this a long time, sitting on my butt whether playing guitar or practicing meditation, it's incredible, in fact I would like to continue buying items from you. I am thinking to purchase an Omni Desk."
—E. B-M. Meditation Teacher, Brooklyn, New York

"Your bench made quite an impression down in Naples, Florida. I am sure that you are going to get more orders, they are all talking about it."
—K.O., Chestland, Ohio

"Dear Peter, The Omni Bench I purchased from you last month is working out very, very well. The medium definitely seems to be the right size, and the Cherry wood is beautiful. Thank you for sharing your gift with us. Many blessings."

—C.C., Northampton, Massachusetts

"Thanks for the bench. It arrived two days ago and looks very nice. The wood is beautiful. Thanks, Peter. I really appreciate your service."
—D.T., San Mateo, California

"Dear Mr. Catizone, I once had one of your wonderful benches. When I was away from home for an extended period of time, somebody relieved me of it, and I have missed it sorely since. I am happy to find your ad in Tricycle. Please send me a bench. Thank you very much — could you hurry? Thanks."
—T.G., Champaign, Illinois

"Greetings Dear Peter, It was great meeting you and talking on the phone. I look forward to many treasured experiences on my new bench. Blessed are you Peter, being the one who markets such great items. Peace and Blessings Always."
—T.

"Greetings Peter, Thank you so much for sending my bench. If it were done any other way I would have probably waited 2 more years. I am living the experience, the bench works wonders, it sends me signals to ensure I get my time in peaceful poise. Thank you, you are truly blessed. And I am sharing your blessing."
—T.G.E., Washington, DC

"Dear Peter, Thank you so much for sending your beautiful bench so promptly. Thank you again — it's beautiful and I'm delighted to own/use such aesthetically pleasing piece of furniture."
—J.D.T., Gouldsboro, Maine

"Peter, The bench is everything you said it was. And a beautiful piece of art too. Thank you."
—A.M.S., Oceanside, California

"It's a beautiful design — thank you."
—L.L., Sydney, Australia

"Dear Peter, Hello once again from central Illinois. I have enjoyed your large Omni Bench very much and really appreciate its craftsmanship and strength. Thank you very much for a fine product.

P.S. I'm just about halfway through a meditation course at IMS in

Barre, MA. Your bench has helped me through this course and how, with my awareness meditations and readings I would like to add your desk to my meditation space. Thanks for your help and care and OUTSTANDING PRODUCTS."
—K.W.K., Springfield, Illinois

"UPS just delivered my bench this afternoon. It's Beautiful. I will take it for a test drive tomorrow morning, which is when I do my daily meditation. I practice the Vipassana style of Buddhist meditation. Thanks again for the beautiful bench."
—S.H., Salinas, California

"Dear Peter, I received my Omni Bench today just in time for my evening sit. Just thought I'd tell you that I love it! Thanks for being such a pleasure to do biz with and thanks for making this wonderful tool."
—C.A., Philippines

"I tried out your product in a bookstore in Santa Cruz and thought it was great compared to a similar seat I have used for two years. I was pleased to find you on the net once I returned to Madison, WI, since I didn't have the space to pack it back from the West Coast. Thanks again."
—M.S., Madison, Wisconsin

"Hello Peter, I ordered a bench from you a while back and I've been very happy with it. I am interested in having a matching desk and bench done."
—A.J.V., Kyoto, Japan

"Thank you — it arrived this morning. It is beautiful and my husband (anniversary gift recipient) loves it. Thanks for such a beautiful and functional product."
—B.R., Clifton Park, New York

"My wife just purchased an Omni Bench for me as a present. It is a wonderful design, much better than the bench I currently use."
—C.D., Clifton Park, New York

"Hi Peter, The bench arrived Monday and it is gorgeous! I love the birdseye maple (I'm guessing). The only problem is I can't admire it when I'm meditating. You are quite a craftsman! Great work!"

—M.V., Billings, Montana

"Dear Peter — Thanks again for trusting me to send you the check for the bench you sent. It came and is great. I am carrying it in my luggage as I travel all year round all over the world. I want another one."
—J.P., Germany

"Dear Peter — My wife recently purchased one of your benches through Yoga Zone. She's thrilled with it as a meditation seat, and I love it, too. Also, I am considering purchasing one for myself. Thanks for your useful product."
—F.C., Berkeley, California

"Thank you for your important work."
—J.R., New York, New York

"I look forward to receiving the desk. If it is anything like the bench, I am sure it is of high quality."
—S.G., Overland, Kansas

"Thank you again for your kind assistance. You've designed a beautiful bench, which has been very helpful to me."
—D.R., L.W., Houston, Texas

"Dear Peter, I am grateful for the gift you are giving the meditation community in general by offering these fine products. Thanks again, your friend and happy customer."
—C.T.S., Lubbock, Texas

"Dear Peter, My desk arrived today. It is lovely."
—K.L.K., Auburn, Indiana

"Dear Peter, I received the benches and desks right on time and in perfect condition. I presented them to my wife this morning and she loved them. They are indeed beautiful works of art. The padouk is really quite extraordinary. Your workmanship far exceeds that of our Santhosh meditation benches. Once again thank you and I will send you business whenever I can. With heartfelt appreciation."
—C.S., Fort Polk, Louisiana

"Peter this is Mary — R.L.'s wife. The bench just arrived today, it's beautiful, it's absolutely beautiful. And it fits perfectly. Thank you very

much. Thank you again it's gorgeous."
—ME.L., Zen Buddhist Temple of Chicago, Northbrook, Illinois

"Dear Peter, Here is the original bench I bought. I want to thank you so much for letting me use it while you make my custom bench. During my week in New York on business, I was able to sit in my hotel room several times and best of all I had just found the Zen Studies, New York Zendo Shobo-Ji which is open to the public on Thursdays and I was able to sit there for the first time, with confidence, because I had my bench with me. It worked out very well. When I get my new bench I plan to always take it to N.Y. with me so I can go to Shobo-Ji and sit in my room. It packed so well in my luggage that it cidn't create any additional hardship at all!"
—K.W., Fresno, California

"Dear Mr. Catizone, Thank you in advance for the Omni Bench. As soon as I saw the picture in Tricycle I knew it was what I arr looking for."
—T.W., Jenkintown, Pennsylvania

"Dear Peter, thanks again for the wonderful desks and benches, we have truly enjoyed them. As a matter of fact, we decided to replace our old benches, and order two more benches from you, one small and one large, made from birdseye maple. As this is your favorite wood, I am really looking forward to using them. By the way, I have a close friend who teaches yoga in Texas, who has several hundred students. I am going to show him your benches when we visit him in April, and hopefully that will generate new orders for you. Thanks again and keep in touch."
—C.S., Fort Polk, Louisiana

"Peter, your bench is a beautiful design, and the wood is also beautiful. Please send me another, a friend wants mine."
—M.P. Associates, Architect, Coral Gables, Florida

"Just got my custom made bench in the mail yesterday. Thank you so very much. The finish and the grain is just beautiful. It looks really great."
—K.W., Fresno, California

"Dear Peter, I received the order today and loved the birdseye maple

and wouldn't trade my bench for the world. Thanks again for everything."
—C.S., Fort Polk, Louisiana

"Dear Peter, Thank you for the Omni Bench. You really ship quickly! I am enjoying it already. Please send me the Omni Desk. I am sure that it will be the same great quality as the bench. Much success in all things."
—H.R., Brooklyn, New York

"It was a couple of weeks ago, but I did receive the very beautiful custom-sized (very large) bench that you made for me. Thank you! It is lovely, and it has the height that I needed."
—L.W., Professor of Environmental Health, Houston, Texas

"Peter — Thanks again. Your work is really marvelous."
—D.D. Ph.D., Kansas City, Missouri

"I just wanted to say how beautiful the bench is, the grain in the figured maple is just gorgeous. I being a musician can really appreciate the quality of the wood. Thanks again, it's just a beautiful piece. It's really great."
—K.D., Asheville, North Carolina

"Absolutely beautiful, I can't wait to try it out."
—R.G., Somerville, Massachusetts

"Hi Peter, The Omni benches have arrived. I love mine, I love the patterning. I don't know whether to look at it, or sit on it. But either way I am going to enjoy it. Thank you very much for creating it. Take care."
—A.A., Santa Fe, New Mexico

"Dear Peter, You have a wonderful way of calming people down! I have the bench in hand, have tried it out and it is perfect. Thank you for your care. It is a beautiful creation, and will certainly enhance my sitting!"
—Mrs. J.T., Windsor, Ontario, Canada

"Hi Peter, The Omni bench arrived yesterday. It is a beautiful piece of work. I am impressed by your attention to detail. Have a great holiday!"

—P.O., Madison, Wisconsin

"My wife just got me the Omni Bench which I was eyeballing for about 5 years. And I just wanted to let you know a couple of things. One is, I am just thrilled with it, the design and the workmanship is something I just don't see very often. It's just magnificent, I love it. God, the wood is just beautiful and the simplicity, I just love it. It's definitely an heirloom. I am going to be spending a lot of time with my bench and I just wanted to let you know that we just love it. Anyway you do great work. Thanks again, and have a good holiday."
—J.K., Anchorage, Alaska

"Peter, The bench and the desk have arrived. They are beautiful. I am really impressed with the grain effects you have achieved. They work really well, as well. When I received them, the first thing I did (of course, after putting the desk together) was sit and write a love letter to my wife of 17 years. Thank you for the wonderful work!"
—J.P., Maidens, Virginia

"Hi Peter! I've been enjoying your Omni Bench. Wonderful craftsmanship! Thanks!"
—D.T., Department of Family Medicine, Madison, Wisconsin

"I was looking at your website, and I have often admired your benches in ads in Tricycle Magazine. I would like to order an Omni Bench. I will try to remain unattached — but I can't wait to receive my custom bench! G.J. Peter hello, This is G.J. You sent me a custom bench. I am so thrilled with it. It looks beautiful. I am very happy with it, and I can't wait to give it a try. Once I give it a little test drive I will be happy to write you my own testimony that you can add to your long list of testimonials, thank you and have a mindful afternoon. Can't wait to try her out tomorrow morning."
—G.J., St. Louis, Missouri

"Peter, I received your bench yesterday, it was just beautiful. I loved it. The color is very soft, not light, and not dark, just very soft. I loved it. The structure of wood is very interesting, but not so sharp. Just silent beautiful. And I definitely like that it's much lighter. Thank you very much, and I am sorry for the inconvenience. You are the beautiful master and a good man."
—H.V., Brooklyn, New York

"Thanks for the prompt reply. And thanks for the prompt shipment!! I had no idea that it would be sent so quickly. Just from the photos (as well as the overall energy of your simple, tasteful website) your benches were by far the best I located, and the ONLY ones I could find incorporating my two essential criteria: legs that are collapsible AND curved at the base. Good job!!"
—A.K., Framingham, Massachusetts

"Peter, Many thanks. I look forward to many hours of comfortable meditation! Take care."
—A.S., Boulder, Colorado

"Dear Peter — I LOVE my Omni Bench! Let me give the Desk a whirl."
—S.W.A., Orange, Connecticut

"Dear Peter: The bench is beautifully made. I love the way that the seat, aided by the curved bottom legs, fits perfectly with my seat. The hinges and the way that the seat folds up is ingenious."
—G.J., St. Louis, Missouri

"Dear Peter — I read in a book somewhere that woodworkers have a weakness for ginger snaps. I hope you enjoy these. Thanks for the extra care. The bench is lovely, and I'm testing it out daily."
—J.A.G., Conshohocken, Pennsylvania

"Peter this is G.C. I ordered the Omni Bench from you which I received and really loved the construction of it. It's just a wonderful bit of old fashion workmanship that you just don't see anymore."
—G.C., New York, New York

"I have a friend here in Hamilton Montana that has one of your benches, and it is wonderful. Please send me one as soon as possible."
—G.N., Corvallis, Montana

"Dear Peter, Again, my thanks for your courteous assistance. And my appreciation for the exemplary craftsmanship of the bench."
—G.C., New York, New York

"Dear Peter, We received the bench and reading table, and they are both beautiful and very well crafted. The quartersawn oak you used matches our two oak bookcases in the same room. And more

importantly, I've already used the bench for a long sitting and sutra reading (with an ill friend very much in mind.) But as I'm getting older and my limbs aren't so limber, the bench is a blessing for longer meditations — and I'll recommend it both to older friends, or to anyone just beginning to practice. Thanks and regards."
—T.S.T., Philadelphia, Pennsylvania

"Got the bench today Peter. It looks lovely and quite tall! Thanks a lot."
—G.C., New York, New York

"Dear Mr. Catizone, The Omni Bench is truly a piece of art and a great meditation aid! I have arthritis in my hip and the Omni Bench is the only way I have found to sit comfortably in meditation."
—C.L., Clifton Park, New York

"I deeply appreciate your work! I've been using my Omni Bench for sixteen years now and still love it and will use it for many more years to come."
—M.K., New York, New York

"Dear Peter: I love the bench and admire the quality and craftsmanship."
—B.L.R., Pittsburgh, Pennsylvania

"Hi Peter, I don't know if you remember me — I'm the fellow from Alaska who ordered a bench from you last December. And what a gem it was. Unfortunately, the Los Alamos fire wasn't so attached to it. That's right, it was burned. On the positive side, I did get to use it in a 20-day vipassana meditation course before its demise. It would have been far more difficult, nay impossible, without it. So, I believe it's time to order another, and hopefully this one will hang around a bit longer."
—C.S., Los Alamos, New Mexico

"Thank you so much for the special customized Omni Bench. You made it exactly to our specifications and it looks like you created another piece of art. Thank you for being so responsive to my needs and for being so generous. You and your craftsmanship will be in all my meditations."
—M.R. — M.K., New York, New York

"I bought an Omni Bench a few years back and I use it every day. I love it."
—W.O., Hyattsville, Maryland

"Peter, The bench is great! Thanks so much."
—B.R., New Haven, Connecticut

"Peter, I am extremely happy with the Omni Bench that I ordered some time ago... thank you for making this high-quality product available. Thanks!"
—M.M., Chicago, Illinois

"Hi Peter, Just a note to say thank you for your Omni Bench. Over a year ago you sent a most beautiful Beech wood bench. All of my body parts love it. Not only is it a pleasure to the eye but to the butt as well. It has added considerably to my practice. For that I thank you."
—J.A.H., Orange, California

APPENDIX 3

Life Lessons from an Italian Yogi

1 Don't mistake kindness for weakness

When I confronted Mendez to stop him from beating Michael, my kindness might have looked like weakness, but it was actually strength. And, as it happened, the purity of my action was rewarded with an intervention, not from God, but for the very real presence of the Boston Police Department.

2 True transformation can happen in an instant, but its effects unfold over a lifetime

That one moment in St. Stephen's changed me forever, but understanding what happened, and appreciating its full value took years. Perhaps your own transformation has already begun, you just haven't seen it yet. Remember that God doesn't just communicate through burning bushes and lightning strikes, and your moment of transformation may be something smaller and subtler, but no less powerful.

3 Sometimes not having a plan is the best plan of all

It's liberating knowing that you don't have to have everything mapped out in order to see, experience, and achieve great things. All my best ideas came without a plan. Body Roc started just because I stupidly bought a consignment of diamonds without knowing what to do with them, and then stuck one on my shoulder. I just followed my instincts and let them lead me where they would.

4 The ability to stay calm in chaos is a superpower

When El Cid held that knife to my throat in the woods, I just said, 'No thanks, I plan to shave tomorrow.' And when that cop held me upside down over the Charlestown Bridge, I stayed calm, because intuitively, I understood that I was safe. That calmness saved my life more than once. Sometimes staying calm under pressure looks like stupidity, and maybe it is. Maybe it flies in the face of all reason to hold your nerve, but as you know, I've never been afraid to make the stupid choice, and I haven't once regretted it.

5 Real strength doesn't come from physical power

I discovered that real strength isn't always about physical power. The wiseguys who came to me after my transformation weren't looking for muscle, they were looking for something much more powerful: connection, understanding and most powerful of all, forgiveness. I think there's more power in understanding and forgiveness than in any other demonstration of strength.

6 The Divine has a sense of humor

Who wants to spend any time in contemplation of a humorless Divine?! Fortunately, my own experience has shown that the Divine likes a good laugh. In my own life, I went from slashing tires to teaching meditation. As unlikely turnarounds go, that's right up there. But life has the capacity to surprise us all if we let it, with its weird contradictions, its misunderstandings, and its embarrassments. When you lean into the madness, life gets easier.

7 As the believer believes

My friend Henry Caruso always took the mayonnaise labels off his jars. When people came over for lunch he delighted them by telling them he had their favorite mayonnaise.

In Hinduism there are three parts of the basic levels of consciousness — Earth, Astral, Causal — the Causal being pure thought and final stage of development before re-uniting with the heart of God.

There will be a celebration for the souls completing the final stages of development. God will then relabel his image as the believer believes. If the believer is Christian, God will relabel as Jesus; if the believer is Jewish, God will relabel as Moses; if the believer is Hindu, God will relabel as Krishna, and so on. Out of love, both God and Henry relabeled their jars to not shock the believer's belief.

8 Your inherited flaws can become your greatest teachers

The violence I inherited from my mother—that hot Italian blood—taught me the value of peace in ways no monastery ever could. It helped me understand and connect with the mafia men who came to me in search of peace and understanding. It caused me to reach out beyond myself in search of whatever else I could be.

9 We are not always who and what we appear to be

Just look at Lobo, the hitman who could show such tenderness. Or me, a street fighter who became a spiritual advisor. It's dangerous to assume that the people we meet are defined by the roles we see them inhabit. In life we can assume many different guises, and wear many different faces. And sometimes, that's the only way we really get to understand who we are, and who we are supposed to be.

10 There's power in laughter

Patients on a hospital ward have always been one my favourites audiences! That's because laughter can be as holy and as healing as prayer. Don't underestimate the power to make someone smile or laugh. It is the greatest leveler in the world. A way of defusing tension or suspicion, or even pain. Above all, it's the best way I know to remind us all that we're all fellow travelers though life.

11 To find your real voice, you must first learn to be completely relaxed

It's the same with finding your true self; you have to let go of who you think you should be in order to reveal who you really are. That person might not be the person you want or expect to find at first. Our egos do a great job of concealing the real versions of the people we need to be, and of obscuring our true path.

12 Start small, and build beyond your wildest dreams

When I built my sculptures, I found that, provided I had the perfect foundation, I could go on to let the wild forms emerge. Life is like that too, isn't it? When you take care of the simple things—your baseline needs—you can let yourself soar. Sometimes, all you need is a cabin in the woods to live your best life. Sometimes, all you need is a bag of rice.

13 Look for the potential beneath rough exteriors

McClosky saw something in that young Italian kid trying to sound like Caruso. Just like I saw something in my wiseguy friends trying to find something of their own to believe in. Even more importantly, you need to find that potential—and that belief—in yourself.

14 To drop the ego, you must first recognize its power

I've said it before—and if you've read this far, you'll know it's true:

I'm a tremendous narcissist! But I think that loving myself is my way of showing how much I love life. Believe me, I'm very much in tune with my frailties, and my wonderful stupidity. And acknowledging that has helped me to look beyond ego, to remind myself that I'm just one part of the great cosmic design.

15 Family patterns repeat until we consciously break them

It's easy to repeat patterns of behavior. Many of my peers followed their fathers and brothers into violence. I could have done something similar. Psychologists refer to this phenomenon as intergenerational transmission or cycle repetition, where behavioral patterns, coping mechanisms, and relationship dynamics are unconsciously passed down through generations.

It takes a lot of courage to break out of the patterns that are expected of us, and follow our own path. But the effort is worthwhile. Living a life freed from other people's expectations is liberating.

16 There's wisdom in unschooled or primitive thinking

Mary used to say she was amazed at what I didn't know, but even more amazed at what I did know. Sometimes too much knowledge can become a cage. And sometimes knowing that you don't know everything is freeing. It's hard work when you're young and you think you know everything. But when you're old, you finally realize you know nothing. And conversely that's when we're at our wisest.

Consider Picasso's admiration for Rousseau's work, which showed how unschooled perspectives can transcend conventional artistic boundaries. This concept echoes the philosophical notion of "beginner's mind" (shoshin) in Zen Buddhism – if you approach situations without preconceptions, it can reward you with deeper insights. The idea also connects to the Socratic paradox: "I know that I know nothing," suggesting that acknowledging our limitations can actually expand our capacity for understanding.

17 Every saint has a past, every sinner has a future

When I learned Thomas Merton was a womanizer, I loved him even more. I saw the things that bound us together. It made him human, relatable. After all, who wants an unrelatable guru who doesn't understand the ways—and the temptations—of the world? Don't feel compromised by what you've done in the past. Don't ever think you can't move beyond the mistakes you've made.

18 The path to enlightenment isn't always straight

My path is still winding on. But every slashed tire, every log in my cabin, and every diamond I meticulously stuck on some model's body were all essential points along the way. The best advice is to take pleasure in the journey. There's no rush. Whether you believe that you are slowly accumulating answers as your lifetimes slip by, or you are living your one life, remember that the diversions along the way can be just as rewarding as the path itself.

19 Enlightenment isn't all Road-to-Damascus moments and lightning strikes

The Divine can reveal itself in ordinary moments too if we're alive to the possibilities, and receptive to the signs. Some of my most profound moments had already been happening all around me before my transformation; I just hadn't seen them. That man who bestowed a kind word on an old lady was such an ordinary, everyday event, but because I hadn't been looking, I hadn't seen any moments like that or appreciated their beauty before.

20 Your greatest challenges can become your greatest gifts

The violence I grew up with led me to search for peace. My mother's chaos drove me to seek stillness. Later in life, my absolute lack of ideas for anything to do with my diamonds led me to find an 'out there' solution. I've also seen how responding to challenges in an authentic way has granted me great gifts. For example, when I stood up to El Cid, or that policeman on Charlestown Bridge; in those moments of extremis, I could have cracked or given in. Being resolute in the face of those challenges made me feel stronger and better about myself.

21 One is essential to the other

Power in transition is relevant to the goal, one being essential to the other. Becoming Vegan was more important to me than being a Vegan because it gave me the opportunity to become something else

(which is why I'm no longer Vegan!)

Tibetan Buddhist monks may be incorrect in their thinking that only the transition / journey is important and not the goal. Because one is essential to the other, and wouldn't exist without the other. They are blatantly disregarding the goal in order to prove a point of being in the moment.

Inconsistency is essential to consistency. You can't have one without the other — they share a symbiotic relationship in their coexistence.

22 Every experience serves a purpose

Looking back over my life, I can see that, from polio, to police chases, to laboring alone on a cabin in the snow, each hardship taught me something valuable about myself, or moved me closer to where I needed to go. We're all so busy living day-to-day that it can be hard to see how all the events that make up our lives might be leading us somewhere. But when you take a moment and assess where you are, those little wrong turns suddenly make sense.

23 The art of the moment

My friend was in love, and I said to her, "Lovers are like sunsets. Each one unique and most glorious in its moment of experience, it will not be your last my dear."

When on stage we follow the moments of script to complete the art of the moment.

24 Don't regret the paths you wish you hadn't taken

In life, you can play many roles, and every role teaches you something new. Being a fighter, an artist, a businessman, and a spiritual advisor all taught me different things. Sometimes their lessons conflicted with each other, and then I had to find the kernels of truth in the margins. Even the 'bad' experiences helped me a little further forwards on my journey.

25 Sometimes you have to kill your darlings

All those months laboring on the log cabin in Oregon, I thought I was building a home for the future. It wasn't until it was finished that it turned out, we had no need of it. In that moment, I knew that all the effort that had gone into its construction meant nothing anymore. And so, I was able to let it go.

26 The path to wisdom often looks like foolishness

Like Yoda in Star Wars, the fool often turns out to be the master. So often, conventional wisdom steers us down cautious paths. If I'd had an ounce of common sense, I wouldn't have done anything in my life. So, embrace your foolishness. Make a virtue of your stupidity and let your wildest ideas lead you where they may.

27 Embrace the stillness and the emptiness

McClosky taught a hard but valuable lesson: I had to learn to let my voice emerge from nothing. I embraced that lesson and let it guide me beyond the lighted stage. So that when I needed to find answers or innovative solutions to problems, I embraced the stillness. I effectively did nothing, and let the answers come to me—unforced— through dreams and meditations.

28 Life itself is the greatest teacher...

... Which is great news for all of us as we grow older! The chaotic, messy, beautiful experience of living gives us all we need. Every failure is a source of great insight. Every man and woman that crosses our path is a potential teacher.

Comments:

catizone@catizone.com

ISBN 979-8-218-68312-2

www.ingramcontent.com/pod-product-compliance
Lightning Source LLC
Chambersburg PA
CBHW071726120626
46550CB00002B/406